Media Production

This book is part of a series published by Open University Press in association with The Open University. The complete list of books in this series is as follows:

Understanding Media: Inside Celebrity (editors: Jessica Evans and David Hesmondhalgh)
Media Audiences (editor: Marie Gillespie)
Media Production (editor: David Hesmondhalgh)
Analysing Media Texts (editors: Marie Gillespie and Jason Toynbee)

This publication forms part of an Open University course *Understanding Media* (DA204). Details of this and other Open University courses can be obtained from the Student Registration and Enquiry Service, The Open University, Milton Keynes, MK7 6YG, United Kingdom: tel. +44 (0)1908 653231, email general-enquiries@open.ac.uk.

Alternatively, you may visit The Open University website at http://www.open.ac.uk where you can learn more about the wide range of courses and packs offered at all levels by The Open University.

To purchase a selection of Open University course materials visit http://www.ouw.co.uk, or contact Open University Worldwide, Michael Young Building, Walton Hall, Milton Keynes MK7 6AA, United Kingdom for a brochure. tel. +44 (0)1908 858785; fax +44 (0)1908 858787; email ouwenq@open.ac.uk

Media Production

Edited by David Hesmondhalgh

Open University Press
in association with The Open University

Open University Press
McGraw-Hill Education
McGraw-Hill House
Shoppenhangers Road
Maidenhead
Berkshire
England
SL6 2QL

email: enquiries@openup.co.uk
world wide web: www.openup.co.uk

and Two Penn Plaza, New York, NY 10121-2289, USA

First published 2006

A catalogue record of this book is available from the British Library

ISBN 0 335 21885 7 (hb) 0 335 21884 9 (pb)

Library of Congress Cataloguing-in-Publication Data

CIP data applied for

Edited and designed by The Open University.

Typeset by The Alden Group, Oxford

Printed and bound in the United Kingdom by The Alden Group, Oxford

1.1

Contents

Series preface

Understanding Media: Inside Celebrity is the first of four books in a series, also entitled *Understanding Media*. The aim of the series is to provide a cogent and wide-ranging introduction to the study of the media. These four books form the central part of an Open University course with the same title (course code DA204). Each volume is self-contained and can be studied on its own, or as part of a wide range of courses in universities and colleges.

The four books in this series are as follows:

Understanding Media: Inside Celebrity, edited by Jessica Evans and David Hesmondhalgh

Media Audiences, edited by Marie Gillespie

Media Production, edited by David Hesmondhalgh

Analysing Media Texts, edited by Marie Gillespie and Jason Toynbee (with DVD-ROM)

The first book introduces four elements central to any investigation of the media (history, texts, production and audiences) via an analysis of the important media phenomenon of celebrity. The next three books in the series then examine texts, production and audiences in greater detail. Across these different topics, the course addresses three *themes* in media analysis, which the course team believe are fundamental to any appreciation of the importance and complexity of the media. These are

- power
- change and continuity
- knowledge, values and beliefs

These elements and themes can be traced via the index of each book, but the book introductions and conclusions will also help follow how they are pursued across the series.

Understanding Media covers a great deal of media studies curriculum, but of course it still isn't possible for us to cover everything. Nevertheless we have aimed to cover a wide range of media examples, both historically and geographically, and to introduce a number of differing and often competing approaches.

The chapters are designed to be rigorous but student-friendly, and we have sought to achieve this in a number of ways. We have provided clear outlines of the aims of each chapter at its beginning, and summaries at the end, with careful explanations along the way. Activities are built into the chapters, and are designed to help readers understand and retain the key concepts of the course. Just under half of these activities are based around *readings* – extracts drawn from books, academic articles and the media themselves – which are integral to the discussion contained in the chapter. These readings are indicated by a coloured line next to the margin. Each book is thoroughly indexed, so that key concepts can be tracked across the different books in the series. Further reading is indicated at the end of each chapter. Finally, although each book is self-contained, references to other books in the series are indicated by the use of bold type.

A fifth book used on DA204 *Understanding Media* has been published by The Open University alone. This book, entitled *Media Technologies, Markets and Regulation*, is edited by Richard Collins and Jessica Evans and is available from OU Worldwide on +44 (0)1908 858785 (http://www.ouw.co.uk).

Media studies has taken its place as a familiar academic discipline in schools and universities, embraced in large numbers by students, but crassly dismissed by commentators who in most cases seem never to have read a serious analysis of the media. The need to think carefully about the media's role in modern societies is as great as ever. We hope that you find these books a stimulating introduction to this vitally important area of study.

Open University courses are produced by course teams. These teams include academic authors, from The Open University and from other institutions, experienced tutors, External Assessors, editors, designers, audio and video producers, administrators and secretaries. The Open University academics on the *Understanding Media* course team were based mainly in the Sociology discipline, within the Faculty of Social Sciences, but we also drew upon the expertise of colleagues in the Faculty of Arts, in order to construct a course with interdisciplinary foundations and appeal. While book editors have had primary responsibility for each book, the assignment of editors' names to books cannot adequately convey the collective nature of production at The Open University. The names of the *Understanding Media* course team are listed at the front of this book.

I'd like to thank all my colleagues on the course team for their hard work and good humour, especially Wendy Lampert, who has been a really excellent and efficient Course Manager.

David Hesmondhalgh, Course Chair
On behalf of the *Understanding Media* course team

The media as symbol makers

David Hesmondhalgh

We are all producers. We all make things every day – even if it is only a cup of coffee, or an email to a friend. Most of us are also involved regularly in the production of symbols – things which stand for other things, such as words, sounds, images. As you read this, millions of people somewhere in the world will be drawing a picture, singing a song, taking a photograph, designing a website, or making up a poem or a story. Some of these people will be paid for what they are doing and some will even be professional symbol makers, attempting to make a living out of entertaining, informing or communicating to audiences.

In more and more countries in the modern world, symbol making is dominated by the media. Most of the entertainment and information that we see and hear comes to us from television, cinema, radio, print or the internet; and one of the core features of the modern world is the huge *asymmetry* between symbol makers and their audiences. Audiences of millions of people regularly consume cultural products made by relatively small numbers of people. Nearly all of us are symbol makers, but very few of us are media producers. This could be taken as an argument that the study of media producers is unimportant compared with the study of media texts, or the study of media audiences, because media producers are a small minority. But, in this book, we take it that it is just as important to study media production as it is any other dimension of the media, and indeed, in certain instances, it is even more so. For if much of the communication that goes on around us is created and distributed by relatively small numbers of people, we surely need to know about these people, about their working practices and conditions, and about how they make the media products which dominate so much of our communicative landscape. This book is an introduction to this area of study.

Our investigation of media production focuses on three themes (as do the other books in this *Understanding Media* series – see the Preface): power; knowledge, values and beliefs; and change and continuity. Let me outline our understanding of these themes, before indicating how the book addresses them, chapter by chapter.

Media organisations do not have a simple one-way influence on audiences but it is indisputable that they have an important role in shaping the knowledge, values and beliefs of people and institutions in modern societies. The media are the means by which we know about the world, from famine and war to the latest sports results; and they also influence the degree to which we think these things matter, and our views of why they happen in the way that they do. Media producers do this via the creation and distribution of television programmes, newspapers, sound recordings, websites, and so on – the texts of modern media. In making and circulating such texts, media producers draw upon knowledge, values and beliefs circulating in the societies in which we live. But media producers also draw on knowledges, values and beliefs at large about the best way to carry out their jobs in the working cultures within which they operate. So a key question for this book is as follows: *how can we understand the relationships between media producers on the one hand, and knowledge, values and beliefs on the other?*

As the media industries have grown, and as more and more symbol production has come under the aegis of the media, commentators have worried about a number of features of the modern communications landscape. Since the media became the basis of big, profit-making businesses from the late 19th century onwards, they have required the kind of investment and organisation that, under the prevailing political and economic systems of that and all eras since, have tended to be provided by wealthy and powerful individuals and institutions. As a result of these developments and concerns, an important question has cropped up time and again in studies of media production, one which forms a second key question for this book: *do the media as a whole ultimately serve the interests of the wealthy and powerful?* This question raises fundamental issues about control over the means of making symbols, and about the power associated with those means. Addressing such issues of power involves looking at what happens in media organisations and at the way in which media work is shaped and experienced. Importantly, it also entails looking at the relationship between media production and media products.

Even though media producers are small in number compared with the media audiences who consume their work, it would be wrong to underestimate the resources that can be mobilised by private businesses and other institutions (such as public service broadcasters) involved in media production. As, in many countries, leisure time has expanded and the disposable income available for consumption of entertainment and information has grown, formidable media industries have evolved, most of them dominated by huge companies alongside many small companies. As these media industries command greater resources, and the largest corporations grow bigger, it could be argued that the asymmetry between producers and consumers grows more skewed. This is just one of the dimensions of change, however, that we need to consider in examining contemporary media production. Some would claim that new media technologies, most notably the internet, have begun to redress this asymmetry. We also need to look at changes and continuities in how media work is organised and experienced, and in how media audiences are understood by media producers. The overall question for the book is: *how are change and continuity intertwined in contemporary media production?*

How do we go about addressing the key questions indicated above? The following chapters address these overarching themes by addressing four crucial issues in the study of media production.

In Chapter 1 John Downey introduces three approaches that offer differing perspectives on media production and the benefits, or otherwise, for societies of changing media systems. These are: the political economy of communication (a radical left political position), market liberalism (a conservative position) and the social market (a 'centrist' position). Downey then shows how these different approaches deal with important and changing aspects of media production (which I touched upon earlier in this introduction): the changing ownership, the growing size and the increasingly global spread of media businesses.

Fierce debates rage between radicals, market liberals and social market centrists over the implications of these processes, and power is central to these debates. Underlying many questions about ownership is the worry that those who own the means of media production will be able to control the production of ideas. Downey shows why political economists are concerned with such issues but also, using the example of *The Simpsons* (a funny and scathing satire of US institutions and mores shown by Rupert Murdoch's conservative Fox Network), why there are no easy equations between ownership and media products. Another key concern in writing on media production has been the way in which large corporations can come to dominate the market for media goods, and whether this may limit the symbol-making which is available to us as citizens, as members of the same social space. To some extent, this concern has been shared by liberals and radicals alike, but with different inflections, as Downey shows. Finally, Downey investigates the internationalisation of the media industries and in particular the massive domination of the global media market by US businesses – does this lead to cultural imperialism or to a more hopeful form of globalisation based on cultural exchange? To illuminate the problem Downey provides a case study of US news giant CNN and the Arabic television station Al-Jazeera.

Downey's chapter stands back from the development of media production over the last two centuries and takes in the big picture. He is in effect asking: *what are the consequences of the massive growth in size and scope of media production in terms of the power of the media and of media producers?* And this is linked to the question of what the media are producing – what texts they make and circulate to us, their audiences.

My own chapter (Chapter 2) addresses the relationships between media producers and media texts in greater detail; it also homes in on the way in which media production is organised. The growth in size and scope of the media industries in the 20th century has led to a complex division of labour. Media production involves not only those people directly involved in media symbol-making – the writers, directors, musicians, actors, journalists, and so on, who tend to provide the 'public face' of media production; hundreds of other people work to get a media product to audiences too. Sound mixers, camera operators, technicians, agents, accountants, marketers, secretaries, printers, cleaners, lorry drivers – all are involved in the making and the circulation of media products.

Over the last few decades sociologists and others have written a great deal about the complex processes involved in media production. This has led to a substantial body of literature about media organisations and institutions, and about what happens within them. A major strand in this work has addressed, explicitly or implicitly, the question of how media texts come to take the form they do, and in Chapter 2 I survey some of this work. I also continue to probe the issues concerning social power and the power of the media which were raised by Downey in Chapter 1, especially in relation to the important fact that we live in a highly unequal world. In research on media production, a crucial corollary of this concern with power and inequality has been a concern with the degree to which media producers act independently of external control or influence. To what extent can media producers create their symbols free from the economic and political preferences of the organisations that are commissioning and distributing their product? To what extent can they operate free from social condemnation or rejection? I survey a number of key studies and explain how they illustrate different views of the relationship between media production and media texts. Are media producers essentially propagandists for the rich and powerful, as two prominent US media activists have argued? Or are the relationships of media producers to sites of social power more mediated and complex than such a view suggests? Studies of crime reporting, rap music and the BBC are used as examples.

One of the key debates in the study of the media concerns the relative power of media producers and of media audiences. While this debate is not directly addressed in this book, it underlies the importance of the area of research discussed by Jason Toynbee in Chapter 3, which looks at how we might understand how media producers conceive of, and gain knowledge about, their audiences. Toynbee begins by explaining how media producers carry out research on audiences, and shows how the US television industry has, over the years, developed mechanisms that provide detailed knowledge of who watches which programmes and with what kind of attention. He then contrasts this 'view from the producers' with two other views. The first is from the political economy approach (the general approach is introduced in Chapter 1) which sees such audience research as a form of manipulation, and a way of delivering packages of people to advertisers. The second is an approach influenced by the French historian Michel Foucault, which sees audience research as a form of *surveillance* of audiences – but ultimately an ineffective one, because it constantly fails to track the audience. Surveying recent changes in market research in the media industries, Toynbee goes on to suggest that audience research practices have increased in scale and complexity in recent years, especially *across* different media. Here we return to the themes of power and autonomy discussed in Chapter 2, for Toynbee suggests that niche marketing and other developments sometimes threaten the independence of creative workers.

Some of the research presented in the first two chapters portrays the institutions of media production as relatively powerful and privileged, compared with audiences or with other aspects of society. But while it is possible to see media producers as privileged in that they get to communicate to the rest of us, and some receive notable fame and wealth, the truth is more humdrum. A tip of glamour rises above the surface, but beneath the waves is a massive iceberg of concealed labour, much of it poorly paid or insecure. A growing literature concerns the working conditions of media workers, and this is explored by Gillian Ursell in Chapter 4. Ursell contrasts four approaches to media work, moving from those based on an economic understanding of such work, to those derived from more sociological perspectives. The first approach is related to the market liberal approach to media production introduced by Downey in Chapter 1, and is derived mainly from management and organisational studies. It examines how media organisations might be made more efficient and/or profitable. The second approach is a radical political one, which sees media workers as exploited. Here Ursell examines some changes in the broadcasting, film and newspaper industries that might support such a view. The third approach is more sociological, looking at certain media workers as professionals and how that status affects their autonomy and working conditions. Finally, an approach influenced by Foucault looks at the 'subjectivities' of media workers and, in particular, at the way in which, in modern societies, media work is generally understood to offer people opportunities for creative 'self-realisation'. Ursell stresses the very real attractions of media work but also the potential pitfalls of work in the sector, including the isolation, stress and uncertainty pointed to by radical critics of work under capitalism.

As should be apparent from this introduction, a major aim of this book is to go behind the scenes of media production. But what is offered is not a *description* of who does what, where and how. Rather, the aim is to show how media production, precisely because it is such an important aspect of the contemporary world, both in terms of the sheer number of people involved in such work and because of the symbolic nature of the products they make, is an area contested by a number of competing perspectives. These competing perspectives provide a variety of explanations of a variety of phenomena, and each carries different *political* implications. In the conclusion to this book, I summarise what each chapter can tell us about the three key themes identified above (power; knowledge, values and beliefs; and change and continuity), and say more about such contestation.

Chapter 1

The media industries: do ownership, size and internationalisation matter?

John Downey

Contents

1 Introduction

The Simpsons has been one of the most profitable, most critically acclaimed and longest running programmes in US broadcasting history. First broadcast in thirty-minute format in 1989, the 350th episode was aired in 2005. For many years, it had a primetime 8 p.m. Sunday slot on Fox, one of the four main US networks; it is widely syndicated in the USA, and has been shown in over 70 countries around the world. The show won, up to 2004, 18 Emmys, the most prestigious US television awards. In its early days it attracted adverse comments from right-wing public figures and politicians. George Bush Senior, during the 1992 presidential election, said that he wanted the USA to be more like *The Waltons* and less like *The Simpsons*. The President did not get it (although if he had done he still would not have approved). The show is a satire of US society, neither an affirmation of its uglier aspects nor a soothing television tale of family values in an era of adversity. Particular objects of contemptuous ridicule are corporate greed, the inanity of network television news, and corrupt politicians. Corporate capitalism, for example, is personified by Mr Burns, a paranoid, ruthless, deeply sinister and control-obsessed character who owns the Springfield Nuclear Power Plant and invites past Republican presidents to his birthday parties.

What is surprising is that the show is broadcast on the Fox Broadcasting Company (2004 revenue $4.55bn), which is largely owned by News Corporation (2004 revenue $22bn), which, in turn, is controlled by the Murdoch family, and patriarch Rupert Murdoch is a right-wing media mogul with a deserved reputation for using his transnational media empire to support favoured politicians and policies. During the 2003 Iraq War, for example, when newspaper and public opinion in the UK was divided over the invasion of Iraq by the USA and the UK, Rupert Murdoch's stable of newspapers unanimously supported the invasion. At the same time, an episode of *The Simpsons* criticised the USA's belligerent foreign policy. Matt Groening, the show's creator, is quite explicit about the implicit politics of *The Simpsons*:

> What *The Simpsons* does is try to see if you can take a genre that nobody takes seriously, and jam in some counter-cultural messages. Now the show is so powerful that when Fox tells us not to do something, we do it anyway. We have Krusty the Klown running for congress as a Republican, and we take Fox News to task and point out what a rabid, right-wing 24 hour spewing [...] station [it] is.
>
> Eliscu, 2002, quoting Matt Groening

The relationship between Fox and the show's producers has rarely been smooth. Initially, in 1985, Fox were interested in buying the copyright of Groening's comic strip *Life is Hell*. Groening, however, was not prepared to sell the rights and came up with the idea of an animated cartoon about a yellow dysfunctional family virtually on the spur of the moment.

It was the huge, early critical and commercial success of the show that strengthened the producers' hands. Not only would a decision by Fox to drop the show have been commercially harmful for the fledgling network, but also attempts to censor would have damaged the already low reputation of the network and News Corporation. This did not prevent Fox from attempting to exercise editorial control. In an episode first broadcast in 1997 an animated Fox employee appeared saying 'As the Fox censor it's my job to protect you from reality'. *The Simpsons* has regularly been critical of the output of the Fox network. Again in 1997, in an episode in which Homer, after one too many *Duff* beers, thinks he has seen an alien, he agrees with Bart that if they cannot get footage of a real alien they will fake it and sell the tape to Fox News. In 2000, the show contained a Fox TV schedule where *The Simpsons* was followed by shows called *Frame-Up!*, *No Pants Island* and *Fart Date*.

The story is a more complicated one than good versus evil, counter-cultural 'cool' versus mainstream 'straights', David versus Goliath, or, indeed, Itchy versus Scratchy. The critique of corporate capitalism does not prevent Simpsons' characters being used to advertise products such as Burger King and it is possible to purchase over 1,000 items of *The Simpsons* merchandising, ranging from Homer fridge magnets to Bart toothbrushes. Despite the desire to remain 'counter-cultural', Groening is now an extremely wealthy and influential member of the US media industry in his own right. The counter-culture has grown up to be rich and influential but the power structures of US society remain deeply entrenched.

Now *The Simpsons* is a not a typical programme. At the end of the 1980s, it is true that animation was not taken particularly seriously and that this opened up some space for political and cultural satire that might not have been permitted in another genre. Also the show's commercial and critical success meant that the producers could target rich and powerful individuals and institutions without fear of permanent unemployment. (This has not always been the case. For example, during the 1950s a Hollywood blacklist operated that prevented left-wing people from working.) What the example does show is that ownership does not determine *everything*. If we wish to understand why media products are as they are, we need to understand the complex relationship between ownership, control and creativity that defies generalisations. It shows the problem of dividing off the study of media production from the study of what media products mean. This division is extremely unhelpful but, alas, very common. Everybody has seen *The Simpsons*. Everybody knows that Rupert Murdoch is a powerful media mogul. How many of us put the two together? ... d'oh!

Pick up a favourite newspaper, book, CD or DVD and look to see who made it. Use the internet to find out something about the company involved. Most company websites contain extensive information for potential investors (for example, annual reports, presentations to business conferences, press releases). You should also try to find independent sources of information regarding the company's activities. Is it a big company? The chances are very high that it will be. In this chapter, we examine differing views of large media corporations. ▪ ▪ ▪

The principal aim of this chapter is to explore some of the issues raised in *The Simpsons* example for media production by:

▪ introducing and contrasting competing approaches to understanding the relationship between media companies, their products (texts) and audiences (Section 2);

▪ discussing whether the ownership and control of media companies affect access of citizens to the means of communication, the diversity of media produced and access to reception (Section 3);

▪ discussing whether company size and market share affect these factors (Section 4);

▪ discussing whether the increasing international spread of the media industries (their *internationalisation*) affects these factors (Section 5);

▪ keeping in mind throughout the implications of these issues for the well-being of individuals and societies.

2 Political economy of communication, market liberalism and the social market

'Political economy of communication', 'market liberalism' and the 'social market' are three competing approaches to understanding the relationship between media institutions and products.

2.1 Political economy of communication

Political economy as an approach to understanding the world was born in the eighteenth century in response to dramatic economic and political change in Europe. What political economists wanted to explain was the emergence of capitalism, a system of economic organisation in which the purpose of production is to make profit, where a minority of individuals own and control the means of production, and where the majority exchange their labour power for a wage or salary. However, political economists wanted not only to understand the emergence of capitalism but also to judge how well or badly it served the interests of society as a whole. In other words, they were interested in both what *was* the case and what *ought* to be the case. They wanted to know what capitalism was like and whether it was any good. That is not to say that all political economists agreed about the answer to either question. While Adam Smith (1723–1790) believed that capitalism would lead to greater equality and freedom, Karl Marx (1818–1883) emphasised what he saw as the inhumane consequences of living in societies divided by class, and advocated revolution to overthrow capitalism in order to bring about greater equality and freedom. Marx's work continues to provide much of the critical inspiration for political economists of communication (Golding and Murdock, 1997). Rightly or wrongly, the notion of a political economy of communication (or of the media, or of culture) has become synonymous with a neo-Marxist approach to media analysis (see Collins, 2002, p.4; **Hesmondhalgh, 2005**).

While political economists stress the power of owners over the production process and over consumers, market liberals tend to emphasise what they see as the economic and political benefits of markets, the autonomy of media workers, the diversity of opinions that may be found in the media and the ability of audiences to interpret and to reject what they are presented with. While for political economists markets are the problem because they create inequality and texts that promote capitalism, for market liberals markets are good because they are not only the most efficient way of producing products that consumers want but also serve to limit the power of the state and thus preserve the liberty of individuals.

Whatever their disagreements, political economists and market liberals both claim to be ultimately concerned with the same thing – what sort of media system is best for 'the people'. By outlining the differences between authoritarian, paternal, commercial and democratic media systems, the British writer Raymond Williams (1926–1988) provided a useful way for thinking more analytically about these issues in his book *Communications* (Williams, 1966). Williams was a critic of both state-controlled and market-based media systems and an advocate of democratic media that would escape the clutches of both. Critics of Williams might accuse him of utopianism. His supporters would argue that without a vision of a better place, of a destination to aim for, we condemn ourselves to reside in un-free and unequal societies.

Reading 1.1 Activity

Read the following extract from Raymond Williams, 'Communications' (Reading 1.1). Compare Williams's four types of media system. Which of these systems best describes the situation of the country in which you live? Take notes on Williams's argument concerning democratic media systems.

Reading 1.1

Raymond Williams, 'Controversy'

The systems

Perhaps it comes down to this: either the communication system is controlled or it is free. In a democracy there can be no argument on this point: the system must be free or there is no democracy. In a free system many of the things produced may be bad or offensive, or may seem bad and offensive to some people. But the only alternative is a controlled system, or monopoly, in which some people are imposing their tastes on others. [...]

In one way, the basic choice is between control and freedom, but in actual terms it is more often a choice between a measure of control and a measure of freedom, and the substantial argument is about how these can be combined. Further, the bare words 'controlled' and 'free' do not seem sufficiently precise, in themselves, to describe the kinds of communication system which we have had or known about or wanted. I believe that we can distinguish four main kinds, and that to describe and compare these will make our thinking about control and freedom more realistic. The four kinds are: authoritarian, paternal, commercial, and democratic.

Authoritarian

In this system, communications are seen as part of the total machine through which a minority governs a society. The first purpose of communication is to transmit the instructions, ideas, and attitudes of the ruling group. As a matter of policy, alternative instructions, ideas, and attitudes are excluded. Monopoly of the means of communication is a necessary part of the whole political system: only certain printers, publishing houses, newspapers, theatres, broadcasting stations will be allowed. Sometimes these will be directly controlled by the ruling group, who will then directly decide what is transmitted. At other times, a more indirect control will be completed by a system of censorship, and often by a system of political and administrative action against sources unfavourable to those in power.

Such a system can operate with varying degrees of severity, and in the interest of several different kinds of society. We can see it in past periods in Britain as clearly as in modern totalitarian states. The distinguishing characteristic of such a system is that the purpose of communication is to protect, maintain, or advance a social order based on minority power.

Paternal

[...] Authoritarians, on various grounds, claim the right to rule. In a paternal system, what is asserted is the duty to protect and guide. This involves the exercise of control, but it is a control directed towards the development of the majority in ways thought desirable by the minority. If monopoly of the means of communication is used, it is argued that this is to prevent the means being abused by groups which are destructive or evil. Censorship is widely used, in such a system, both directly and indirectly, but it is defended on the grounds that certain groups and individuals need, in their own interest and in the public interest, protection against certain kinds of art or ideas which would be harmful to them. Where the authoritarian system transmits orders, and the ideas and attitudes which will promote their acceptance, the paternal system transmits values, habits, and tastes, which are its own justification as a ruling minority, and which it wishes to extend to the people as a whole. Criticism of such values, habits, and tastes will be seen as at best a kind of rawness and inexperience, at worst a moral insurrection against a tried and trusted way of life. The controllers of the paternal system see themselves as guardians. Though patient, they must be uncompromising in defence of their central values. At the same time, the proper discharge of their duty requires a high sense of responsibility and seriousness. At different times, and serving different social orders, the paternal system can vary in the degree to which it explicitly announces its role or explains its methods. The actual methods can also vary widely: sometimes putting the blanket over everything; sometimes allowing a measure of controlled dissent or tolerance as a safety-valve. But the general purpose and atmosphere of the system remain unmistakable.

Commercial

The commercial attitude to communication is powerfully opposed to both authoritarianism and paternalism. Instead of communication being for government or for guidance, it is argued that men [sic] have the right to offer for sale any kind of work, and that all men have the right to buy any kind that is offered. In this way, it is claimed, the freedom of communication is assured. You do not have to ask anybody's leave to publish or to read. Works are openly offered for sale and openly bought, as people actually choose.

In its early stages, and in some of its later stages, such a system is certainly a means to freedom by comparison with either of the former systems. But since this freedom depends on the market it can run into difficulties. Can a work be offered for sale if there is no certainty that people will in fact buy it? When production is cheap, this risk will often be taken. When production is expensive, it may not be. In a modern system of communications many kinds of production are inevitably expensive. [...] [P]ractical control of the means of communication, over large areas and particularly in the more expensive kinds, can pass to individuals or groups whose main, if not only, qualification will be that they possess or can raise the necessary capital. Such groups, by the fact of this qualification, will often be quite unrepresentative of the society as a whole; they will be, in fact, a minority within it. Thus the control claimed as a matter of power by authoritarians, and as a matter of principle by paternalists, is often achieved as a matter of practice in the operation of the commercial system. Anything can be said, provided that you can afford to say it and that you can say it profitably.

Democratic

We have experienced the other three systems, but the democratic system, in any full sense, we can only discuss and imagine. It shares with the early commercial system a definition of communication which insists that all men have the right to offer what they choose and to receive what they choose. It is firmly against authoritarian control of what can be said, and against paternal control of what ought to be said. But also it is against commercial control of what can profitably be said, because this also can be a tyranny.

All proposals for new systems appear abstract, and at times unconvincing, because it is only when they are put into practice that they can be felt to be real. The working out of any democratic system will obviously be long and difficult, but what matters first is to define the general nature of a cultural system compatible with democracy, since there is only any chance of success in building it if enough of us can agree that this is the kind of thing we want. [...]

On the right to transmit, the basic principle of democracy is that since all are full members of the society, all have the right to speak as they wish or find. This is not only an individual right, but a social need, since democracy depends on the active participation and the free contribution of all its members. The right to receive is complementary to this: it is the means of participation and of common discussion.

> The institutions necessary to guarantee these freedoms must clearly be of a public-service kind, but it is very important that the idea of public service should not be used as a cover for a paternal or even authoritarian system. The idea of public service must be detached from the idea of public monopoly, yet remain public service in the true sense. The only way of achieving this is to create new kinds of institution.
>
> *Reading source*
> Williams, 1966, pp.123–9 ▪ ▪ ▪

Commercial systems, Williams argues, with their emphasis on production for profit and freedom to produce and consume, initially offer greater freedom than the authoritarian systems that they traditionally replace. One of the best recent examples of this is the reorganisation of the media in Central and Eastern European states after the revolutions of 1989 (see Figure 1.1). Here the control of respective Communist parties over the means of communication has been partially replaced by a market-based system. Although governments still often seek to control the means of communication directly, the citizens of these countries now have access to a greater range of analysis and opinion than before. The move to the market has brought greater freedom than in the authoritarian past but such a situation is not good enough for Williams. Williams argues that we have not yet experienced a democratic media system. In such a system we all would have the right to transmit and the right to receive independent of our income or our political views. The only way of achieving this, according to Williams, is to create new kinds of institutions that rely neither on capitalism nor on the state.

2.2 Market liberalism

Friedrich von Hayek (1899–1992), one of the twentieth century's most persistent and articulate advocates of the benefits of the market and the dangers of socialism, lived long enough to enjoy the fall of the Berlin Wall. Hayek (1994/1944) argued two things: that free markets are the most efficient way of allocating resources, thus ensuring economic vitality and prosperity; and that markets are the best way to ensure freedom and democracy as they provide a plurality of views and prevent the state from restricting the liberty of individuals in society. While Hayek, especially in the 1930s and 1940s, often felt that he was writing against a consensus that advocated state planning and intervention, his ideas have become increasingly accepted in the last 20 years or so. They are now seen as 'common sense' just as a greater role for the state seemed to be

Figure 1.1 *Crowds demolish the Berlin Wall in 1989*

commonsensical for much of the twentieth century. Market liberal views are commonly found in financial papers and periodicals (such as the *Financial Times*, *The Economist* and the *Wall Street Journal*) and in right-wing think-tanks (such as The Adam Smith Institute, The American Enterprise Institute, The Heritage Foundation, The Cato Institute). Wilson (2003), for example, makes a case for the end of public service broadcasting and all regulation of television content in the UK in favour of free market competition. While such a market liberal take on the media is vigorously contested in the UK within academic and political elites by social marketers and political economists (Curran and Seaton, 2003, pp.392–414), such views are 'especially well-entrenched in the United States' (Curran, 2002, p.218) where they have had a clear and continuing impact on policy formation since the early 1980s.

2.3 Social market approach

If the political economy approach sees the free market as antithetical to freedom and equality, and the market liberal approach sees markets as essential for their existence, the social market approach steers a course between the two. On the one hand, it is wary of the degree of control that states may wish to exercise over the operation of the media. On the other, it recognises the threat that media markets may pose for pluralism. As a consequence, the social market perspective advocates a mixed economy approach of private and public media (Curran, 2002, pp.217–47).

The social market perspective is broad in scope – some place more emphasis on the role of the state and some on the market. It is possible, for example, to derive a social market position from the work of Adam Smith who is often associated with a market liberal position (Green, 1995, p.33). Smith argued not only for free markets but also for universal state provision of education so as to enable all in society to make rational judgements concerning the issues of the day. In our age the media industries are an important way in which people are informed about all aspects of life and thus it could be argued that the state should step in to ensure that citizens poorly served by the media market are catered for. This may include negative regulation (for example, to ensure that no-one controls all of a nation's newspapers) and positive regulation (for example, that television news coverage is objective and politically impartial) of both private and public media. The intention behind this position is to capture the benefits of the market (efficiency, dynamism, independence from the state) and state provision (programme diversity, universal access) while mitigating their dangers.

In order to explore further the differences and similarities between these three approaches, I will address three questions that have been central to the study of media making: Does ownership matter? Do size and market share matter? Does internationalisation matter?

3   Does ownership matter?

Political economists of communication believe that ownership matters because those who own the means of production will also be able to control the production of ideas. According to Marx (who was not a political economist of communication, but who inspired many writers who take this approach):

> The class which has the means of material production at its disposal, has control at the same time over the means of mental production ... Insofar as they rule as a class and determine the extent and compass of an epoch, they do this in its whole range, hence among other things they also regulate the production and distribution of the ideas of their age: thus their ideas are the ruling ideas of the epoch.

Marx and Engels, 1974/1847, pp.64–5

Note that what interested Marx was less the actions of individual owners than the behaviour of owners collectively as an economic class and as a social class across history. While individual owners might be in competition with each other to a certain extent in order to secure higher profits, this limited competition pales into insignificance, he argues, compared with the fundamental agreement of those individual owners concerning how society ought to be organised in order to protect their interests as a class: for example, the agreement of these individual owners concerning the desirability of private property rights. A problem with this approach is that it assumes that the capitalist class is relatively homogeneous in terms of ideas. It may be relatively homogeneous but, if it is, this needs to be shown through empirical analysis. Empirical analysis may also reveal substantial disagreements.

While Marx examines class behaviour, Hayek's pro-market approach to economy and society looks at individuals. While Marx sees capitalists working together to promote their collective interests, Hayek sees competition between individuals in order to make profit. Markets, according to Hayek, are self-regulating. If individuals think that they can make a profit then they will enter the market. If they do not they will not. Thus markets will ensure that individuals do not become too powerful as they need to satisfy the needs of consumers in order to become profitable and they are always subject to competition from other entrepreneurs. Markets find a spontaneous order through the balancing of supply and demand. The collective interests of society, Hayek contends, are best served by self-interested individuals competing against each other rather than through 'planning' (see Figure 1.2).

3.1 Watchdogs or lapdogs? Media and power

Although Marx was fundamentally concerned with analysing classes rather than individuals, if we find out who owns and controls some of the biggest media firms then we cannot help but be struck by the continuing power of certain individuals and families. The most striking example is that of Silvio Berlusconi in Italy. At the time of writing,

THE ROAD TO SERFDOM

THE ROAD TO SERFDOM

❸

The "Planners" promise Utopias . . . .

A rosy plan for farmers goes well in rural areas, a plan for industrial workers is popular in cities—and so on. Many new "planners" are elected to office

❹

but they can't agree on ONE Utopia

With peace, a new legislature meets; but "win the war" unity is gone. The "planners" nearly come to blows. Each has his own pet plan, won't budge.

Figure 1.2 A pamphlet version of Hayek's ideas, published by General Motors in the 1940s, explained his views of the dangers of state planning

Berlusconi is Italy's wealthiest person and became Prime Minister in May 2001 (he previously occupied the same position for a few months in 1994). Berlusconi made his fortune originally in property investment and construction before moving into media industries in the mid-1970s. A total absence of effective media regulation enabled him, in 1978, to establish a national private television network; thereafter he continued to build a media empire with the help of Bettino Craxi, leader of the Italian Socialist Party and Prime Minister of Italy from 1983 to 1987. By the late 1980s Berlusconi controlled three private television networks as well as the largest book and magazine publishing house in Italy. In 1993, with the traditional Italian parties of government mired in corruption scandals and faced with the possibility of the left-wing parties forming a government, Berlusconi formed a new party, Forza Italia, in a matter of weeks. The party lacked any form of internal democracy, with many candidates drawn from Berlusconi's business concerns. After the March 1994 election, Berlusconi formed a coalition government with the Lega Nord and the Alleanza Nazionale, two far-right, openly xenophobic parties. This administration was short-lived but Berlusconi returned to power with the help of the same coalition partners in May 2001. At the time of writing, the Berlusconi family own 96 per cent of Fininvest, a holding company that in turn owns nearly 49 per cent of Mediaset's shares. Mediaset runs three television networks (Canale 5, Italia Uno and Retequattro), which together have a 45 per cent audience share and account for 60 per cent of total television advertising sales.

Public television in Italy has also traditionally been carved up between political parties. Before the 1993 breakdown of traditional political parties, the Christian Democrats, the strongest political party, controlled RAI1, the public service channel with the largest audience, the Socialists controlled RAI2 and the Communists RAI3 (which, incidentally, was beset by transmission problems that restricted reception). From 1996 to 2001 the centre-left government controlled RAI1. After the 2001 election Berlusconi moved to banish what he saw as the left-wing bias of television. Using their parliamentary majority to appoint the governors of RAI, RAI1 became the province of Forza Italia, RAI2 the province of Lega Nord, while the centre-left's control of RAI3 was weakened. Popular presenters critical of Berlusconi have been sacked and RAI news programmes have been careful not to anger him.

Activity 1.2

Examine the photomontage of Berlusconi and the Italian Fascist leader Mussolini, given in Figure 1.3. What do you think is its message? How valid is this message in your view? ■ ■ ■

The photomontage in Figure 1.3 suggests that Berlusconi has the same kind of absolute power as Mussolini did in 1930s Italy. While Berlusconi is undoubtedly extremely influential in terms of media control, that does not stop millions of Italians protesting on the streets against his policies and poking fun at his regular gaffes. This would suggest that his power is far from total. Moreover, the Italian case is extreme. Berlusconi is unusual in that he is a media mogul turned politician. Without the systemic corruption crises that beset Italian politics in the early 1990s he might have remained a wealthy tycoon with friends in high places.

Figure 1.3 'Total war on the government of the new Duce Berlusconi.' This poster, produced by the Italian Marxist-Leninist Party, features Silvio Berluconi and the Italian fascist leader Benito Mussolini, who like Hitler, called himself 'Leader' – 'Il Duce' in Italian

If we look beyond the specificity of the Italian case and the personalities involved, however, we can see broad similarities across developed capitalist societies. A good deal of commercial media across

North America and Europe are clear in their support of policies to create a less state-regulated, lower taxation, free-trade, pro-business economy. While it is easy to set up Murdoch, Berlusconi and others as bogey-men, by focusing too much upon individuals we might miss broader economic and ideological movements that are transnational in scope. Political economists argue that, in contrast to the market liberals' notion that free-market media act as watchdogs over the activities of the state, right-wing media attempt to bring about governments amenable to free-market policies and then seek to ensure their longevity. Big media and neo-liberal governments are seen as accomplices and not adversaries.

Many of the largest international media companies are 'publicly' owned (they are listed on a stock exchange, and their stocks are owned by a variety of shareholders) and not dominated by an individual or a family. Shareholders may be individuals but are often large institutions that may choose to invest their money by buying shares. These large institutions often get their money from members of the public. Pension funds, for example, receive money from individuals who hope to receive a return on their investment in order to provide for retirement. Shareholders ultimately possess power in the company. The greater the percentage of a company's voting shares one owns the greater say one has in terms of the overall direction of the company. Market liberals, therefore, argue that there has been a broadening of share ownership and, as a result, ownership is not concentrated in the hands of a relatively small number of individuals. Political economists, on the other hand, point to the vastly unequal distribution of wealth in capitalist societies and the tendency for such inequalities to widen since the early 1970s.

Market liberals and some social market writers respond that, in the mid twentieth century, 'a managerial revolution' brought about a dilution of the power of owners (Berle and Means, 1968). According to this view, the public character of many media companies (that is, stocks are listed on a stock exchange) means that the ownership of the company is effectively separated from the control and management of the company and therefore the owners cannot use their economic power to influence the character of the products produced. Thus there is a separation of powers that prevents owners or managers from becoming too powerful. Professional managers, according to this line of argument, are concerned with the bottom line rather than with spreading political messages and thus focus on satisfying the needs of consumers and resist ideological interference from shareholders.

Political economists raise two objections to this. Firstly, they say, it underestimates the amount of control that owners do still exercise. While the day-to-day operational running of the company may be left in the hands of managers, the owners still make the fundamental decisions that determine the direction of the company. The owners retain, in other words, allocative control and may use this power to serve their political as well as economic interests (Murdock, 1982). Secondly, while managers and owners might play different roles in the running of a company, it is highly likely that managers will be drawn also from the relatively wealthy and privileged classes of society and thus the link that Marx suggests between the control of the means of production and the production of ideas is not broken. Publicly owned companies and the separation of function between owners and managers tend to make the picture more complex, but political economists argue that the 'managerial revolution' does not fundamentally alter it.

3.2 Market power to the people?

A further market liberal criticism of political economy's claimed link between economic control and the character of media texts is that this view tends not to recognise that firms must satisfy, or at least promise some satisfaction of, the desires of consumers in order to make a profit. The behaviour of firms is seen as driven by the demands of consumers, and firms can only make a profit when they provide consumers with what they want rather than with what the companies want. There is something in this argument. Consumers do have *some* market power but this is far from the full story. It underestimates the power of media firms to decide what to bring to this market. Very importantly it skates over the influence that advertisers have over media products that are often reliant upon advertising revenue. Most commercial television operates through broadcasters selling advertising space and hence they will attempt to broadcast programmes that are attractive to advertisers. Advertisers are customers whose needs have to be met as well.

We may imagine a situation in which the production of a media text is clearly in the interests of citizens and yet it does not get made – telling the truth and making a profit may be incompatible. Here, market-based media would be at odds with the existence of well informed citizens. In a market-based system, the pre-eminent criterion as to whether or not a product is made is profit. This is problematic when a product has other properties that may benefit citizens (it may be true or beautiful) but is not thought to be potentially profitable and therefore remains unmade. All the potential benefits of these 'merit goods', to use an economist's description, are lost (see Congdon, 1995, pp.15–17 for a similar argument from a social market perspective influenced by the work of Karl Popper on the open society). On the other hand, if the state controls the media or even if it just exerts influence on public service media, then it is also possible that citizens will be kept in the dark. This has led social marketeers to advocate a mixed economy of privately owned and public service media in order that they can act as a check on each other. Supporters of such a mixed system argue that the presence of public service media forces commercial media to raise their game as they have to compete for audiences with products not made according to the profit motive (Collins, 2002). Of course, such a system might also lead to the people being misled by both!

By and large, market liberals tend to put more faith in 'the people' knowing what they want and being able to resist media manipulation (that is, being rational agents) than do political economists. When it comes to the media, however, it is unwise either to assume that consumers know exactly what they want or that they are dupes. Films are not like pop-up toasters. When we want a pop-up toaster we have some clear idea of what we want: an electric appliance that heats up bread, makes it brown in a reasonably short period of time and informs us that the toast is toast by 'popping up' the slices of bread. Films, however, can be very different from each other and in order to know which films we like the best or find most useful, enlightening or amusing we need to have the ability to see as many different films as possible. Because it is very difficult to know what certain films may do for us before we see them, if we do not have access to those films then it does not make sense to say that we know what we want as consumers.

Claims that consumers know what they want also rely on an abstract and unrealistic notion of the power of consumers. It is abstract because it does not take into account how consumer tastes are previously shaped by the media texts on offer and how the choice available to consumers is limited by decisions made by media firms concerning what and what not to produce. For example, I like gangster films but I only know this because I have seen many of them and I have only seen many of them because film production companies have found it to be profitable to produce such films. If they had not decided to produce gangster films then it would not have been possible for me to like them or it might even be difficult for me to imagine that I might like them. In other words, the decisions made by media firms about what to produce limits the choice we have. We form our preferences from a limited menu, hence Homer's copious consumption of Duff beer.

Media firms tend to make profits either through selling products directly to consumers or through selling access to audiences to advertisers. Both rely on consumers having enough disposable income either to buy the product or to interest the advertisers of another product. Media products in a market-based system will tend, therefore, to be aimed at those consumers who possess large amounts of disposable income and who may be easier to reach in terms of the delivery of products, while poorer and/or geographically distant citizens have to make do with fewer products from which to choose. This means that the inequalities of society are reproduced in market-based media systems.

In response, market liberals often take public service media to task for cultural elitism (Compaine, 2001). The claim here is that markets provide what citizens want while the state provides what it thinks the citizens should want. Once the state starts to control the people rather than the other way round, democracy flies out of the window. Market liberals argue that commercial media are accountable to the public through the market (consumers can withhold their business) while public service media are often funded, as in the UK, through a license fee that is a form of compulsory regressive taxation, and are only very indirectly accountable to the public.

In contrast to Marx's confident association of ownership with ideas, it is not clear that capitalist-owned media produce texts that simply legitimate the power of this class. The capitalist class may be confused about what their interests are and the people who are hired to produce media texts may have some degree of autonomy from both owners and managers. Are *The Simpsons* Rupert Murdoch's favourite television family? Despite the money they have made him, I doubt it. While the political economy approach is very good at analysing economic and political power, political economists have been less adept at analysing media texts. Thus the relationship between ownership and text is often assumed rather than demonstrated. This points to the need to be cautious about making sweeping statements, the need to argue the case text by text, and to supplement economic analysis with an analytical toolkit that may help us understand and explain the meaning of media texts. *The Simpsons* may be read as a critical text and may serve to show that texts are not necessarily in cahoots with the views of their owners, but one swallow does not make a summer. Berlusconi and Murdoch may allow some critical comment on their channels simply to demonstrate their democratic credentials. How diverse are media texts really? The market liberal position often assumes diversity, the political economy position often assumes homogeneity, and the actual meaning of media texts slopes off out of frame.

4 Do size and market share matter?

Market liberals and political economists both believe that the market share of companies making up an industry matters. If one company dominates the market for a good then it is said to have a monopoly. This company, as it does not have competitors, can control supply of the product in order to maximise profit. If a few companies dominate the market then it is said to be an oligopoly. The UK national newspaper market may be described as an oligopoly, for example, because four companies control 90 per cent of sales. The behaviour of oligopolistic companies is difficult to predict. Oligopolistic markets may be more or less competitive depending on circumstance. Neo-liberal economists argue that, in contrast to monopolies and oligopolies, perfectly competitive markets with a large number of companies competing in the market will be the most efficient, and will yield maximum utility to consumers. A perfectly competitive market has the following characteristics:

- a large number of small producers and consumers in a given market;
- none of the producers and consumers can influence the price on their own;
- goods and services are easily substitutable for one another (that is, the products produced are the same);
- all resources are perfectly mobile (for example, resources for investment in order to enter the market are readily available);
- transaction costs are zero;
- the intersection of demand and supply determines price.

Very few markets approach perfect competition. Market liberals and political economists disagree about the extent to which media markets diverge from perfect competition and to what extent this divergence actually matters. As we saw earlier, market liberals stress that media markets are competitive and at the service of consumers while political economists tend to emphasise how companies use their market power to the detriment of citizens' interests.

One must be careful here to distinguish between different media markets. Markets will differ, for example, depending on the height of entry barriers. If people think that internet publishing offers the prospect of large profits, then there will quickly be new entrants to the market because of the relatively low start-up costs (the dot.com boom, bubble and burst of the late 1990s is a good example). The same is not true for the film industry because of the expense of making and distributing a film, although small-budget independent films do occasionally make big box-office returns. Even if a media market is an oligopoly (that is, dominated by a few firms) it is very hard to predict the behaviour of firms. Sometimes they get pally with one another to ensure that they all make a good return, for example, by scheduling the release of blockbusters so that they do not clash with one another. Sometimes they try to cut each other's throats through price wars in the hope of driving competitors out of business and thus of putting themselves in a position to make more profits later on (as Rupert Murdoch's News International attempted to do with a price war in the UK national press market in the 1990s).

The products of media and communication industries resemble what economists call 'public goods'. A good is public if its consumption by one person does not result in a lowering of supply to others. A film, for example, can be watched by millions of people without affecting its future supply. The cost of the first copy of media products tends to be high while the marginal costs of media products tend to be low (the marginal cost is the cost incurred when an additional unit of the product is produced). For example, a film might cost $100 million to produce. The costs of production (fees for actors, directors, equipment, props) are incurred whether or not the film is successful at the box office. Because first copy costs are generally high and marginal costs low, the obvious strategy to maximise profits is to show the film to as many consumers as possible. Big is beautiful from the perspective of media firms wishing to maximise profits. Large media firms enjoy economies of large scale and will tend to be more successful than smaller firms who will often be taken over by competitors (this is known as horizontal integration) or will leave the market.

Media firms may also pursue a strategy that exploits economies of scope. Here media firms search for greater profits by diversifying their range of products and services within a value chain. For example, film production companies may expand into film exhibition or video sales or a cable film channel. The high first-copy costs are also important here. If film companies have invested a good deal of money in making a film then it makes sense if the aim is profit maximisation to sell the product in as many formats as possible. This helps to explain the growth of film soundtracks, DVDs, merchandising, and so on. Through reducing transaction costs along the value chain, media conglomeration may also result in economic efficiency beneficial to the consumer (Doyle, 2002, pp.37–41).

4.1 Hollywood: from Fordism to post-Fordism

The history of the Hollywood film industry is an excellent example of how an industry can evolve while still being controlled by a small number of players. Up until 1914 film production was geographically dispersed in the USA. Between 1914 and 1920 production came to be concentrated in Hollywood, California. The industry was initially characterised by a large number of producers and exhibitors but, by the 1920s, because of horizontal and vertical integration, eight studios controlled most production, distribution and cinemas (Paramount, Twentieth Century Fox, Warner Brothers, Metro-Goldwyn-Mayer (MGM), Radio-Keith-Orpheum, Universal, Columbia, United Artists). The era of the studio system lasted until the 1950s. Studios tended to specialise in particular genres, central producers controlled a large number of creative projects, films were made in the companies' studios and creative talent tended to be contracted to the studio for extended periods. In other words, film production in studios, at this time, resembled production in car factories. This system of production is often called Fordist.

However, two shocks to this studio system occurred in the late 1940s. Firstly, the vertically integrated studios were forced to give up their exhibition arms by a 1948 Supreme Court anti-trust ruling. Secondly, the rise of television led to an initially dramatic reduction in the number of filmgoers. The studios responded to these shocks with a strategy of cost-cutting, risk-spreading and innovation. In essence, major studios worked out that film production was becoming riskier and decided to transfer some of the risk to independent producers. This led to an increase in the number of independently produced films. In 1960, 28 per cent of films were made by independents with 66 per cent made by major studios. By 1980, 58 per cent of films were produced by independents. This has led some to argue that Hollywood became a post-Fordist industry characterised by product differentiation, outsourcing of production to specialist contractors and geographical dispersion of production (Christopherson and Storper, 1989).

While there is some truth in this, it must not be forgotten that the majors still dominate the film industry but they do so less through the control of production and more through the control of the *circulation* of films – control of the process by which they get to their audiences (cf. **Hesmondhalgh, 2005**). Independents remain subservient to the major companies because of the majors' control over the circulation of films and because of their financial clout. While independent production companies play a very important creative role in film production, the production and release of these films are dependent upon striking a deal with a major either for a completed film (known as a negative pick-up because the major buys the negative of the finished film), for production finance or for distribution. The vast majority of commercially successful films in the USA are distributed by Warner Brothers, Fox, Universal, MGM, Paramount, Sony, New Line and Buena Vista. Some of the old majors had been joined by Sony (who bought Columbia in 1989), New Line (part of the Time Warner group) and Buena Vista (part of Disney). Except for MGM all of the majors are now part of larger media conglomerates. While a large number of independent producers exist, they are dependent upon the media conglomerates that control distribution and that have effectively reasserted control over exhibition by owning television networks, cable channels, video and DVD sales companies and cinemas. Since the 1980s, the growth of such conglomerates has been helped by state deregulation of the media and cultural industries in North America and Western Europe (Wasko, 2003).

The advantages of large media corporations are accentuated because of the very high risks involved (see **Hesmondhalgh, 2005**, and Chapter 3 in this book). It is extraordinarily difficult to predict which films, television shows and recorded music will be commercially successful and which not (a fact that should lead us to be cautious about arguments that emphasise the all-conquering power of media conglomerates). A large majority of media products will make a loss and a small minority will make large profits. While larger companies can withstand lean periods, smaller companies will often go to the wall. What we see, therefore, is a self-propelling industry structure in which it makes sense for media firms to get bigger and bigger in order to exploit scale and scope and spread risk.

In 2001 the US entertainment industry magazine, *Variety*, published a list of the top 50 'global' media firms by revenue (global media is a highly dubious concept bearing in mind that significant proportions of the world's population do not have access to electricity, not to mention televisions). The top six, all multimedia conglomerates – Time Warner, Walt Disney, Viacom, Vivendi Universal, Bertelsmann, News Corporation – had a combined revenue in 2000/1 of nearly $147bn. The top six accounted for over 51 per cent of the total revenue of the top 50. Of the top 50 global firms 24 are based in the USA, seven in Japan, five in the UK, three in Germany, two in France and one each in Luxembourg, Australia, Denmark, Sweden, Argentina, Italy, Mexico, Canada and Brazil. While all of the firms are international they tend to concentrate on either particular geographical markets (for example, Bonnier in northern Europe) or markets where there is a shared language (for example, Televisa in the transnational Spanish-speaking market). The exceptions to this are the larger firms who have film and television production facilities and seek to distribute their products beyond particular geographical areas or language markets. The large majority of the revenues of these firms, however, are still derived from North America and Europe, although as living standards in Asia rise the media conglomerates are eager to exploit opportunities for profit.

4.2 Are media conglomerates good for you?

Is the growth of large international media conglomerates good or bad for citizens? Political economists argue that the domination of an industry by a few large players may lead to a less than fiercely competitive environment in which higher prices are paid for media products. They argue that large media conglomerates use their economic power to arrange marketing and merchandising deals through other large companies such as Burger King or McDonald's. The customers of Burger King and McDonald's (two powerful and ubiquitous international organisations) will be exposed to images and experiences of these media products, such as *Star Wars*, *Tarzan* or Mickey Mouse. This works to the benefit of the larger companies and puts smaller media companies at a disadvantage. They are, therefore, less likely to be able to successfully compete with these products. So the size of the media conglomerates behind products such as Mickey Mouse, *Tarzan* and *Star Wars* gives them a distinct competitive advantage (see Figure 1.4).

In addition, although oligopolistic markets may lead sometimes to ruthless competition between the large firms as they seek to kill each other off (and consumers may benefit from this at least in the short term), nevertheless, horizontal and vertical integration may lead to a reduction in the number and type of media products on offer as large firms follow conservative product strategies (for example, the rise of the blockbuster and the sequel). In the end, political economists claim, media conglomeration leads to a worsening of a culture that sustains democracy by limiting the range of products produced and the access of audiences to those products.

Market liberals, in contrast, argue that larger media companies occupying dominant market positions are often in a better position than smaller companies to take creative risks because they know that they can survive short-run commercial failure. Fewer, stronger firms may lead to greater product diversity and lower prices to consumers as conglomerates enjoy both economies of scale and scope and may pass on some of these

Figure 1.4 *The collaboration of powerful transnational companies such as McDonalds and Burger King give certain media products a distinct competitive advantage*
Source: © 2005 McDonald's Corporation. © Disney. © 2005 Burger King Corporation. © 2005 LucasFilm Ltd.

savings to the consumer. Whether or not this is so is a question that is obviously open to empirical analysis.

The rise of conglomerates has coincided in certain media industries (for example, recorded music) with a strategy of product differentiation in which companies seek out profitable niche audiences. Additionally, a changing technological environment has led to the remarkable development of digital cable and satellite television that has led to the provision of greater diversity, at least for audiences able and willing to pay for it. There is no simple causal link, market liberals argue, between media conglomeration and a reduction in the type of products brought to market.

Indeed, those advocating a market liberal approach towards the creation of media conglomerates argue that there are benefits to be had to consumer welfare as a result of conglomeration. Economies of scale and scope may mean lower prices for the consumer. Also the bringing together of different firms may allow, as AOL argued when taking over Time Warner, more rapid technological progress, ultimately benefiting the consumer either in terms of price, choice or both. Market liberals also argue that media conglomeration has not led to a loss of diversity in terms of the products available to the consumer and here the empirical evidence tends to support their case. Einstein, while distancing herself from a market liberal perspective, shows that the repeal in the USA of rules limiting the transmission by television networks of programmes they themselves produced has not led to a reduction in programme diversity (Einstein, 2004), though it has led to the reassertion of network-produced programming in place of independent production. In addition, it is often argued that the advent of the internet, because of its relatively low entry costs, means that we should not be so concerned about media concentration in television, music or film (Compaine, 2001).

Political economists tend to skip over research that suggests that greater media concentration in terms of ownership does not necessarily lead to a loss of programme diversity, and instead make the *prima facie* credible assertion that more concentrated ownership leads to product homogenisation (McChesney, 1999); or they argue that it is the market itself rather than the existence of big media that restricts diversity – thus pointing towards the desirability of positive regulation and publicly funded media (Einstein, 2004). The question here is not really 'are media conglomerates good for us?' but rather a more fundamental one: 'are free markets good for us?' Political economists are also sceptical about whether the internet really delivers diversity for all. Large television news providers dominate the provision of news on the internet. While the internet may be a relatively cheap way of disseminating news, the costs of collection and production remain the same, thus playing into the hands of powerful established news providers. Also the internet is not accessible to all; a digital divide exists both within rich countries and between poor and rich countries.

5   Does internationalisation matter?

Let us now look at the third of the three principal questions we are dealing with in this chapter. Internationalisation of the media refers to a process whereby media ownership, production and consumption spill over the borders of nation states, thereby raising the question of whether one nation may dominate another culturally through the exportation of media products.

The US writer Herbert Schiller's groundbreaking work of the 1960s and 1970s, written from a political economy perspective during the Vietnam War, saw media and cultural exports as the ideological arm of US imperialism. It is undoubtedly the case that the US political, military and cultural establishment after the Second World War saw Hollywood cinema as a key way of exporting US values, thus making the world safe for capitalism, liberal democracy and US hegemony (Dower, 1999; Wagnleitner, 1994). While Schiller saw US imperialism and cultural imperialism as malevolent, market liberals celebrate US primacy and the universal benefits of exercising 'soft power', citing as examples the role that US popular culture played in inspiring the revolutions in Central and Eastern Europe in 1989 and US-based satellite channels in Iran (Nye, 2004). The differences between Schiller and Nye are essentially ethical and political in character, stemming from competing assessments of the benefits of US 'empire' or 'primacy'.

Reading 1.2 Activity

In 1992, in a new edition of his book *Mass Communications and American Empire*, Herbert Schiller reflected on events since the first publication of the book in 1969. Read the extract from these reflections and take notes on the following question. How, according to Schiller, has cultural imperialism changed since the 1960s?

Reading 1.2

Herbert Schiller, 'A quarter-century retrospective'

Mass Communications and American Empire was written between 1965 and 1967 and first published in 1969. Seismic shifts in the balance of world power have occurred since those years. Yet the world preeminence of the US media/cultural sphere remains intact, if not more secure than ever. The war in the Persian Gulf in 1990–1991 provides a recent measure of this preeminence.

In that war, a new dimension of information monopoly and control was demonstrated. The messages and imagery that circulated nationally and worldwide were transmitted by *one* network: Cable News Network (CNN). CNN, in turn, acquired its material essentially from two sources, the Pentagon and the White House. As a consequence, most of the world's understanding of what was happening in the Gulf and what it signified came from practically a single U.S. source. [Mowlana et al., 1992]

How has this incomparable capability – the power to define – been sustained and *augmented* over the past quarter of a century? No less important, what differentiates the 1990s from the mid-1960s with respect to media-cultural influence? [...]

Internationalization of the corporate perspective

The corporate voice now extends far beyond continental limits, just as corporate operations no longer are contained within national territory. Powerful U.S. companies have used their considerable resources, in collaboration with their overseas counterparts, to achieve internationally the operational arrangements they enjoy at home. Accordingly, deregulation that was launched in the United States in the late 1970s moved across the ocean and soon became the major thrust of Thatcherism in England. Now it thrives on the continent as well. The movement is especially strong in the communication sector.

Not so long ago, communication in Western Europe was the exclusive domain of the state. In recent years, in one country after another, for example, England, France, Italy, and Spain, transnational and national corporate interests have privatized and liberalized (commercialized) state broadcasting and telephone services.

In varying degree, similar transformations have been effected in Latin America, Asia, and Africa, under similar stimuli. Freedom for the corporate voice, and especially for its marketing message, has been the common development in most parts of the world. Hailed, not unexpectedly, by corporate-dominated channels of information as the triumph of freedom, the benefits from these changes have gone overwhelmingly to the big global corporate companies. The paramount benefit has been the formidable growth of capital's worldwide power and at the same time the weakening of its opposition – labour, organized as well as unorganized. Corporate media-cultural influence has been no less enhanced.

There is another striking change. Whereas in the 1960s it was accurate to refer to American media and cultural imperialism, in the 1990s the term and the concept have to be recast. Twenty-five years ago,

U.S. media products flooded the world. Today, there is no diminution of American popular cultural exports. In fact, the dollar and physical volumes of the outputs of the U.S. cultural industries flowing into the international market are higher than they were then.

What has changed is that the producers of these products have become huge, integrated, cultural combines. These conglomerates, which include film, TV production, publishing, recording, theme parks, and even data banks, now offer what amounts to a total cultural environment. And they offer it to a global as well as a national market. Actually, the global market is increasingly considered in the decisions of the big cultural industry corporations. Consumerism is no longer an American phenomenon with some spillover effects. It flourishes and is rooted in Europe, Japan, and numerous other enclaves around the world.

In addition, the cultural conglomerates now are not exclusively American owned. German, Japanese, French, Brazilian, English, and other national capitals increasingly are invested in these transnational enterprises. For this reason, U.S. cultural styles and techniques – acknowledged as the most popular internationally – have themselves become transnationalized, serving the ideological and marketing needs of capital, wherever its origin. The *Los Angeles Times*, for example, reported, 'Euro-TV turns to Hollywood. New commercial networks on the Continent recruit U.S. writers, producers and directors to develop and guide shows. A major goal is to sell the program in America.' [Tempest, 1991] [...]

Half a world away, in the same vein, a Brazilian researcher noted that Brazilian television programming is 'the creolization of U.S. cultural products. It is the spiced up Third World copy of Western values, norms, patterns of behavior and models of social relations.' His findings, no different from what one would conclude in the United States or Europe, is that 'the overwhelming majority of Brazilian soaps have the same purpose as their U.S. counterparts, i.e. sell products' [Oliveira, 1990].

Selling products is, above all, the role of popular culture in an age of transnational corporate market domination. 'Local' sponsors for Brazilian programming have familiar names: Coca-Cola, Volkswagen, General Motors, Levi's, and so on.

What these accounts confirm is the global advance of consumerism, promoted and spearheaded by the transnational corporate system, with its cultural-media sector at the leading edge. Corporate capital, insistent on full access to the informational system to propagate its commercial and ideological messages, has demanded, and achieved, the privatization of the communication sector (telephone, television, satellite, and computer) in one country after another. In France, for example, 'television ad[vertising] spending tripled from 1985 to 1990.' At the same time, French commercial interests still are not satisfied because, they say, 'the biggest problem may be that the Government has tended to view television not as a business, but as a cultural asset' [Neher, 1991]. It is clear that this archaic view needs to be overcome if France is to be truly and fully culturally conglomeratized.

This problem of France's has never existed in the United States. Radio and television, from their inception, were regarded, and used, as profit-making opportunities, despite some dissenting voices. Still, Europe seems to be overcoming its 'problem.' In 1990, though European advertising revenues had already reached an unprecedented peak, an American consultant company, Booz-Allen & Hamilton, Inc., bullishly reported: 'On a per-household basis, four times as much is spent in the United States on television advertising as in Europe.' The European potential, therefore, is 'enormous' [Bruce, 1991, p.1].

What has been happening over the past twenty-five years, the past ten especially, has been a phenomenal expansion of transnational capitalism and its seizure of global communication facilities – nationally based, to be sure – for its marketing and operational and opinion-controlling purposes. American cultural imperialism is not dead, but it no longer adequately describes the global cultural condition. Today it is more useful to view transnational corporate culture as the central force, with a continuing heavy flavor of U.S. media know-how, derived from long experience with marketing and entertainment skills and practices.

References

Bruce, L. (1991) 'Europeans tune in to a new wave of television', *International Herald Tribune*, 11 June, p.1.

Mowlana, H., Gerbner, G. and Schiller, H.I. (eds) (1992) *Triumph of the Image: The Media's War in the Gulf – A Global Perspective*, Boulder, CO, Westview Press.

Neher, J. (1991) 'The battle over French TV: profits vs culture', *New York Times*, 12 August, p.C-8.

Oliveira, O.S. (1990) 'Brazilian Soaps Outshine Hollywood: Is Cultural Imperialism Fading Out?' Paper presented at the meetings of the Deutsche Gesellschaft fur Semiotik, Internationaler Kongress, Universitat Passau, October 1990.

Tempest, R. (1991) 'Euro-TV turns into Hollywood', *Los Angeles Times*, 11 July.

Reading source

Schiller, 1992, pp.1, 11–15 ■ ■ ■

Schiller argued that the pre-eminence of US media and cultural industries had been augmented since the 1960s. A prime example of this, he claimed, was the role played by CNN (Cable News Network) in the 1990–91 Persian Gulf War. CNN, run from Atlanta, Georgia, and reliant upon the White House, the State Department and the Pentagon as news sources, presented to the world nothing less than the US establishment view of the war. For Schiller, what changed since the 1960s was that producers of this 'cultural imperialism' became integrated into conglomerates and that these conglomerates were not exclusively owned by US citizens. This internationalisation of ownership and production, however, has not been accompanied by an internationalisation of styles. US cultural styles and techniques have become the *lingua franca* of transnational capitalism (see Hardt and Negri, 2000).

In this context, we might look in more detail at CNN. Cable News Network was launched by media entrepreneur Ted Turner in 1980. It was the pioneer of the 24-hour rolling news service whose format has been copied around the world. CNNI (International) was launched in 1985 but rose to prominence in 1989 because of the massacre of rebellious students in Tiananmen Square in China and the revolutions in Central and Eastern Europe. The popular appetite for immediate, exciting event-based news was confirmed during the Gulf War where real-time images of the events were broadcast internationally. CNN, at the time of writing, has a network of around 150 correspondents, 42 international bureaux and 23 satellites, can reach 236 million households worldwide and estimates its potential audience to be 1 billion. Its regular audience is only a small fraction of this but CNN viewers are often wealthy and powerful people. It is also, since 1996, part of Time Warner. Although CNN has some 'local' content aimed specifically at particular countries, continents, or language markets, the Atlanta headquarters retains strict editorial control. During the 2003 UK and US invasion of Iraq, for example, a leaked CNN memo revealed that all journalists must submit their scripts to Atlanta for approval. Critics of CNN accuse the network of being in the pocket of the US state and of transnational corporations. After the 1991 Gulf War it emerged that CNN had allowed Pentagon employees to work in its newsroom.

In contrast to the cultural imperialism thesis, some politically liberal commentators suggest that CNN has become an important actor influencing international relations and the behaviour of governments (Volkmer, 1999). This is known as the 'CNN effect'. Advocates of this position point to the growth of 'humanitarian intervention' by organisations such as the United Nations and the North Atlantic Treaty Organisation (NATO) (examples cited here are intervention in Northern Iraq in 1991, Somalia in 1992 and Kosovo in 1999) and argue that intervention was prompted by emotive real-time television coverage that affected both public opinion and politicians. While proponents of the cultural imperialism thesis see CNN as the Pentagon's very own news service, politically liberal commentators see CNN as a global watchdog pricking the conscience of US politicians.

Even though the ownership of media conglomerates has become more international, it is clear that the USA dominates the content and style of international media trade. World trade in cultural goods quadrupled between 1980 and 1998 to nearly $400bn. The USA has an 85 per cent share of the global film market and 68 per cent of global television exports. At a time when the US generally imports far more than its exports in other goods and services, its exports of media products far outweigh imports. The USA's trade surplus in audiovisual products with the European Union (EU), for example, has grown from $3.5bn in 1993 to $6bn in 1998 to $8.2bn in 2000. Additionally, increasing numbers of media firms in the EU are controlled by US-based companies.

Stop and reflect for a moment on US dominance of the global media industries. Make a list of factors that may have helped the USA to dominate global media in this way. ■ ■ ■

One important factor behind the domination by the US of global media markets is simply that the USA has a large population. While there is greater income inequality than in other advanced capitalist societies, the average income is very high by international standards. That means that there are a very large number of people with large amounts of disposable income. These are, of course, ideal market conditions for media industries that either generate revenue through subscription or advertising or both.

The size of the US media market gives it a competitive advantage internationally. In contrast to a political economy analysis of this preponderance, the social market perspective (which is often adopted by political liberals, as opposed to market liberals) explains the USA's position through reference to the notion of cultural discount (Hoskins et al., 1997). Cultural discount is where the product of one country does less well internationally than it does domestically for reasons of cultural difference. If we assume that the same cultural discount applies to Hollywood films and French films, that both films cost the same to produce, and that they were both marketed internationally, the revenues of the Hollywood film would be much greater than those of the French film because of the size of the US market. US firms can then use this domestic strength in international markets. National cinemas with large and culturally distant domestic markets have generally been more successful at establishing a thriving film industry. Examples here include India, Hong Kong and Nigeria.

There is also here a tendency towards upsizing. The higher the budget of the film, the greater the difference between the profits of the US film and those of the French film, assuming a positive relationship between budget and audience numbers. This means that it is very difficult, for example, for national film industries in Europe to compete with Hollywood internationally and so they mostly aim to produce lower-budget films for the domestic market or for an international niche market. In 2003, the average cost of a US major-produced film was $63.8m compared with $16.8m in the UK, $4.2m in France and $2.3m in Italy (European Audiovisual Observatory, 2004).

One should also consider that a strategy of the US film and television content industry has been to reduce cultural discount by either incorporating local elements in the marketing of products or telling stories that travel well by playing down the specific character of US culture. Indeed, one could speak of cultural accumulation rather than cultural discount for many US products. As many viewers outside of the USA have become accustomed over the course of the twentieth century to the high budgets, special effects and stars of Hollywood cinema, domestically produced films are often perceived to be either of a lower quality or for a niche arthouse audience. As a consequence, Hollywood studios have increased their control over international markets. In 1985 Hollywood film had a 41 per cent audience share of the Western European box office; by 1995 this had grown to 75 per cent before falling to 71 per cent in 2002. The Hollywood majors in 2000 earned half of their revenue from overseas compared with 30 per cent in 1980 (Miller et al., 2001).

Most of the USA's media products are produced in English. While not the biggest market in terms of people, it is the biggest in terms of income. We would expect that cultural discount would be lower in same language markets and so US products enjoy once more a competitive advantage. This is true also for UK media products. The fact that English is a widely spoken second language and/or business language also helps to reduce cultural discount. The UK, for example, is the second largest global exporter of television programmes with nine per cent of the market in 2002. While the English-speaking market is the most lucrative internationally, media conglomerates are increasingly turning their attention to markets in Asia (by 1998 China was the third largest importer of cultural goods) and Central and Eastern Europe.

Media conglomerates are often accused by political economists of using their market power to restrict competition internationally. It is true that some US firms offer to sell their goods to international markets at a lower price than in the USA. Having made a profit domestically, a US company may choose to sell a product more cheaply in international markets. While this may not be the best way to maximise profits in the short run, it may be so in the longer run by discouraging domestic producers from entering the market as they would not be able to compete on price with the US imports. Another way in which media conglomerates use their market power is to insist that television channels purchase a slate of their products. They are not prepared simply to sell the popular box-office films to broadcasters.

From a market liberal perspective, the internationalisation of ownership and the expansion of trade in cultural goods is a good thing. More trade promotes economic efficiency as economies specialise in producing the goods and services that they are best equipped to produce: the ones that they enjoy a comparative advantage in producing. From this position, concerns about the impact of cultural imports on national identity are misplaced. The building bricks of market liberalism are individuals not nations. There is no reason why nations ought to survive and, therefore, no justification for protectionist measures. According to the market liberal position, if people wish to have locally produced media in addition to US-produced media, as they tend to, then they will pay for it.

The US dominance in the trade of media products, together with the cultural and growing economic and political importance of media industries and the persistence of national identities, has meant that media trade issues have been hotly disputed internationally. Concerns about the USA's domination of the world film industry have been expressed in Europe since the 1920s for a variety of reasons relating to issues of control of national identity. During the rise of political anti-Semitism in 1920s Europe, Hollywood was viewed with suspicion because of the number of Jews who were in the industry. In Britain, objections were raised that Hollywood films were critical of the British Empire (Trumpbour, 2002, p.28). While the reasons may have changed since then, the source of concern has remained.

The European Union, for example, practises a form of protectionism with respect to audiovisual products. The *Television without Frontiers* (TVwF) Directive, which came into operation in 1989, stipulated that there should be an internally free market in the EU and, where practicable, over 50 per cent of an EU television station's content should originate in the EU. This, of course, is another way of saying that under 50 per cent should originate in the USA. The goals of this directive were to promote the European audiovisual industries and to foster cultural diversity.

There is, however, a possible contradiction between the creation of an internally free market and the fostering of cultural diversity as one would expect larger EU states such as the UK, France and Germany to dominate the European market at the expense of smaller states. The TVwF Directive also assumes that both cultural diversity and the creation of a European cultural identity through television are good things and will be promoted through the imposition of quotas (for a discussion of these and related issues see Collins, 2002). Both sets of assumptions are certainly worthy of debate. It is highly likely that cultural protectionism will remain a central part of EU audiovisual policy. While the EU adopts a social market position, the USA advocates a market liberal approach with regard to international trade of audio-visual products.

While the USA obviously exports more media products than it imports, the cultural imperialist thesis has been subjected to sustained critique (see Tomlinson, 1991; **Gillespie, 2005**). A number of arguments are put forward:

- The description of imbalances of cultural trade as imperialism is inappropriate because, historically, imperialist projects were carried out through the exercise of both economic and coercive power. With cultural trade the coercive element is not present.

- The concept of cultural imperialism overestimates the relationship between state coercive power and the behaviour of media firms. It is wrong to speak of a military–industrial–entertainment complex as media firms are independent of state interests.

In addition, according to its critics, the cultural imperialism thesis tends to:

- Focus on analysing the actions of the powerful states and media firms and ignores the actions of the 'colonised'. This overlooks both questions of consent and resistance.

- Assume that all US or 'Western' media products are similar in terms of their promotion of corporate capitalism and liberal democracy whereas they are diverse in terms of the beliefs and values that they promote.

- Assume that the audience laps up uncritically the views expressed in the imported media products, and to underestimate both the powers of creativity and critique of audiences.

- Romanticise non-Western cultures and demonise Western cultures.

- Overlook the activities of domestic media industries both as industries and as critics of imported cultures.

- Overlook the degree to which the 'colonised' export their cultures to the coloniser via trade of goods and migration of people.

Partly as a consequence of these criticisms of the cultural imperialist thesis, the concept of globalisation has come to the fore in academic, journalistic and political discourse. If cultural imperialism means cultural imposition, globalisation means cultural exchange. The idea of an imposition of a monolithic culture has been replaced by the idea of cultural syncretisation and the creation of hybrid identities. While there is some validity to this change of thinking, it is worrying that advocates of cultural globalisation often overlook how economic and coercive power are intimately related to media power and the maintenance of local and global inequalities (Golding and Harris, 1997). From the political economy perspective, the concept of 'globalisation' is an ideological screen behind which cultural imperialism continues to operate.

5.1 Cultural imperialism and cultural globalisation: the case of Al-Jazeera

A case study of Al-Jazeera helps to illuminate the strengths and weaknesses of the 'cultural imperialist' and 'cultural globalisation' theses. Arab states are strategically important to the USA because of their oil reserves. Since the Second World War, US foreign policy has been based around support for Israel and for authoritarian regimes that would contain the threat of Communist revolution. Since the 1970s Islamic fundamentalism has become a new threat to US dominance, first in Iran with the overthrow of the US-backed Shah in 1979, but also in other important Arab states such as Saudi Arabia and Egypt. The popularity of Islamic fundamentalism poses a threat to the US-backed regimes and the USA is presently encouraging such regimes to embrace reform in order to ward off further Islamic revolutions and to establish US hegemony. US foreign policy is widely denounced in the 'Middle East' as imperialistic. One could argue that this is a consequence of US policy. One could also argue that the USA's relative weakness in this region in terms of 'soft power' is also an important factor to consider.

'Global' Hollywood, for example, derived in 2001 only 1.1 per cent of its overseas film and tape rental revenues from the Middle East (including Israel), compared with over 15 per cent alone from the UK, for reasons to do with cultural difference and widespread poverty (Scott, 2004, p.54). Hollywood films have also tended to arouse as much opposition as identification in Arab societies since the 1920s. Even those people who like the idea of 'the American dream' may argue that it simply highlights the gap between the rhetoric and the reality of US foreign policy. In addition, since winning independence from France and Britain, Arab regimes have sought to control their media systems directly. While imports of US soaps and serials abound, news programmes tend to be critical of the USA and Israel (Ayish, 2002). To combat this, the USA has recently launched Radio Sawa and a satellite television station, Al Hurra, aimed at the burgeoning disaffected Arab youth population and offering a diet of US popular culture and pro-US news. Whether the USA will succeed in winning hearts and minds is, however, an open question. Similar attempts have failed before (Vaughan, 2002).

Al-Jazeera is often called the Arab CNN (El-Nawawy, 2002). The 24-hour news channel came to prominence in the West after the attacks on New York City and Washington DC on 11 September 2001, as it was Osama Bin Laden's preferred means of communication (US television networks succumbed to state pressure and refused to broadcast Bin Laden's videotaped messages). The reputation of the channel grew during the US military campaign in Afghanistan when it was the only television station with a base in Kabul and it was criticised by UK and US governments for its reporting of the invasion of Iraq and subsequent occupation. Al-Jazeera offices have been bombed and reporters killed by US forces. It is unclear whether or not this happened intentionally. The channel is increasingly subject to a variety of censors (the New York Stock Exchange rescinded journalistic accreditation for reasons of space, Datapipe refused to host the Al-Jazeera website after a series of hackings, and the US-appointed Iraqi Governing Council expelled an Al-Jazeera journalist for supposedly inciting violence).

Al-Jazeera was launched in 1996 after the BBC's Arab service was shut down when its Saudi backers pulled out because of a BBC documentary critical of human rights abuses in Saudi Arabia. Many of Al-Jazeera's reporters were trained by the BBC and other Western broadcasters. The channel is based in Doha, Qatar. It is available to 35 million households in 22 Arab countries and has 10 million subscribers outside of the Arab world (numbers of viewers are hard to estimate given the extended nature of many Muslim families and the collective character of much television watching in cafés). The station is making increasing and successful efforts to reach the Arab diaspora (there are estimated to be seven million Arabic speakers in Europe, four million of whom subscribe to Al-Jazeera, and two million in the USA, half of whom are subscribers). Eighty-seven per cent of British Asians have access to Al-Jazeera via BSkyB. Most of Britain's 1.6 million Muslim population, however, do not speak Arabic. This means that the audience share of Al-Jazeera is very small in the UK. As well as adopting CNN's style and format, plans are afoot to launch an English language Al-Jazeera channel primarily aimed at non Arabic-speaking Muslims (for example, there are 140 million non Arabic-speaking Muslims in Pakistan and 200 million in Indonesia) (Hodgson, 2003). An Arabic website, Aljazeera.net, was launched in January 2001. In 2002 there were 811 million page impressions and 161 million visits to the site, placing the site among the most popular 50 sites worldwide. In 2003 an English language version of the site was set up.

Al-Jazeera prides itself on its independence. After the end of colonialism, Arab states saw television as an instrument of propaganda and developed authoritarian media systems. Certainly, Al-Jazeera has been critical of many regimes in the Arab world as well as condemning policies of the Israeli and US governments. The channel has made many enemies in high places and is regularly accused of being an agent of the CIA, Mossad (the Israeli secret police), Saddam Hussein, Al-Qaeda, and of being anti-Jewish and inciting violence.

Al-Jazeera appears, however, to be remarkably independent. This is so despite the fact that it is bankrolled by the Emir of Qatar (a small state of roughly 700,000 inhabitants), while his cousin (who is, incidentally, the foreign minister) owns 35 per cent of the shares. The independence and particularly the criticism of US foreign policy are even more impressive given Qatar's open and material support of the USA's invasion of Iraq in 2003.

Activity 1.4

Visit the CNN and Al-Jazeera websites and contrast the reports about the present conflict in the Middle East of these 'impartial' news organisations. Does CNN promote US foreign policy interests and the interests of corporations? Whose interests are served by Al-Jazeera's reports? Think back to Williams's typology of media systems in Section 2.1. Where would you fit Al-Jazeera and CNN? ■ ■ ■

This suggests that commercial media systems are developing in parts of the world where authoritarian systems were previously dominant. But, at time of writing, Al-Jazeera's financial position appears to be highly precarious. It is dependent upon an annual subsidy from the Emir. The channel is not profitable despite its popularity because of the unwillingness of corporate advertisers to use the channel; they are wary of offending both Arab and Western regimes that are regularly criticised in its programmes. The Al-Jazeera budgets are consequently lower than, for example, CNN. Its main newsroom in Doha is less than 150 square metres and it has only 755 employees compared to CNN's nearly 4,000. Perhaps cultural imperialism still prevails?

6 Conclusion

In Reading 1.1, Raymond Williams claimed that what matters, in practice, is whether a media system is more controlled or more free. The more free the system, the greater are the opportunities for citizens both to produce and to receive a diverse range of media products. The more free the system, the greater are the opportunities for individuals and societies to develop and reach their full potential. The more free the system, the greater the prospects of fostering both artistic creativity and a participatory democratic culture. Whenever we study media industries, we should be striving to answer the fundamental questions: How free are they? Who are they controlled by? Whose interests are being served? These are questions that are motivated by an ethics of freedom and equality.

To answer these questions we need to adopt a holistic approach and to think about different forms of power: economic power (which may be wielded by a corporation) and coercive political power (which may be exercised by the state), as well as media power, which is associated in complex and often contradictory ways with both economic and coercive political power. Such issues of power are explored further in the next chapter.

Further reading

Croteau, D. and Hoynes, W. (2001) *The Business of Media: Corporate Media and the Public Interest*, Boston, Pine Forge. A well informed introduction to the issues discussed in this chapter. The authors' opposition between 'corporate media' and 'the public interest' has been criticised by some for lacking nuance.

Curran, J. (2002) *Media and Power*, London, Routledge. A collection of essays that addresses the complexity of the different positions discussed in this chapter, recognises their strengths and weaknesses, and develops an original argument.

Einstein, M. (2004) *Media Diversity: Economics, Ownership, and the FCC*, London, Lawrence Erlbaum Associates. A book showing that, while fewer firms do not necessarily mean less diversity, limited diversity is a consequence of free-media markets. This market failure, the author argues, points to the need for media regulation.

Hesmondhalgh, D. (2002) *The Cultural Industries*, London, Sage. A comprehensive and highly readable introduction to the cultural industries – the core of which are the media industries.

Hoskins, C., McFadyen, S. and Finn, A. (1997) *Global Television and Film: An Introduction to the Economics of the Business*, Oxford, Clarendon. A book written by economists that is comprehensible to non-economists and which, by seeking out economic explanations, challenges cultural imperialist accounts of the media industries.

Schiller, H. (1992) *Mass Communication and American Empire* (2nd edn), Boulder, CO, Westview Press. A passionately written book by a leading advocate of the cultural imperialism thesis.

References

Ayish, M. (2002) 'Political communication on Arab world television: evolving patterns', *Political Communication*, vol.19, pp.137–54.

Berle, A. and Means, G. (1968) *The Modern Corporation and Private Property*, New York, Harcourt Brace.

Christopherson, S. and Storper, M. (1989) 'The effects of flexible specialization on industrial politics and the labor market: the motion picture industry', *Industrial and Labor Relations Review*, vol.42, no.3, pp.331–47.

Collins, R. (2002) *Media and Identity in Contemporary Europe*, Bristol, Intellect.

Compaine, B. (2001) *The Myths of Encroaching Media Ownership*, OpenDemocracy Limited, www.opendemocracy.net/(accessed 7 February 2005).

Congdon, T. (1995) 'The multimedia revolution and the open society' in Congdon, T., Graham, A., Green, D. and Robinson, B. *The Cross Media Revolution: Ownership and Control*, London, John Libbey.

Curran, J. (2002) *Media and Power*, London, Routledge.

Curran, J. and Seaton, J. (2003) *Power without Responsibility: The Press, Broadcasting, and New Media in Britain* (6th edn), London, Routledge.

Dower, J. (1999) *Embracing Defeat: Japan in the Wake of World War II*, New York, Norton.

Doyle, G. (2002) *Understanding Media Economics*, London, Sage.

Einstein, M. (2004) *Media Diversity: Economics, Ownership, and the FCC*, London, Lawrence Erlbaum Associates.

Eliscu, J. (2002) *Homer and Me*, Rolling Stone, www.rollingstone.com/(accessed 7 February 2005).

El-Nawawy, M. (2002) *Al-Jazeera: How the Free Arab News Network Scooped the World and Changed the Middle East*, Boulder, CO, Westview Press.

European Audiovisual Observatory (2004) *Focus: World Film Market Trends*, Marché du Film, www.obs.coe.int/online_publication/reports/focus2004.pdf (accessed 7 February 2005).

Gillespie, M. (2005) 'Television drama and audience ethnography' in Gillespie, M. (ed) *Media Audiences*, Maidenhead, Open University Press/ The Open University.

Golding, P. and Harris, P. (eds) (1997) *Beyond Cultural Imperialism*, London, Sage.

Golding, P. and Murdock, G. (eds) (1997) *The Political Economy of the Media*, vols.1 and 2, Cheltenham, Edward Elgar.

Green, D. (1995) 'Preserving plurality in a digital world' in Congdon, T., Graham, A., Green, D. and Robinson, B. *The Cross Media Revolution: Ownership and Control*, London, John Libbey.

Hardt, M. and Negri, A. (2000) *Empire*, Cambridge, MA, Harvard University Press.

Hayek, F.A. (1994/1944) *The Road to Serfdom*, Chicago, University of Chicago Press.

Hesmondhalgh, D. (2005) 'Producing celebrity' in Evans, J. and Hesmondhalgh, D. (eds) *Understanding Media: Inside Celebrity*, Maidenhead, Open University Press/The Open University.

Hodgson, J. (2003) 'The Arab CNN goes global: revenue-starved Al Jazeera needs to break out of Arab world', *Observer Business Pages*, 7 September, p.8.

Hoskins, C., McFadyen, S. and Finn, A. (1997) *Global Television and Film*, Oxford, Clarendon.

Marx, K. and Engels, F. (1974/1847) *The German Ideology*, London, Lawrence and Wishart.

Tomlinson, J. (1991) *Cultural Imperialism: A Critical Introduction*, London, Pinter.

McChesney, R. (1999) *Rich Media, Poor Democracy*, Urbana and Chicago, IL, University of Illinois Press.

Miller, T., Govil, N., McMurria, J. and Maxwell, R. (2001) *Global Hollywood*, London, BFI.

Murdock, G. (1982) 'Large corporations and the control of the communications industries' in Gurevitch, M., Bennett, T., Curran, J. and Woollacott, J. (eds) *Culture, Society, and the Media*, London, Routledge.

Nye, J.S. (2004) *Soft Power: The Means to Success in World Politics*, New York, Public Affairs.

Schiller, H. (1992) *Mass Communications and the American Empire* (2nd edn), Boulder, CO, Westview Press.

Scott, A. (2004) 'Hollywood and the world: the geography of motion-picture distribution and marketing', *Review of International Political Economy*, vol.11, no.1, pp.33–61.

Trumpbour, J. (2002) *Selling Hollywood to the World: US and European Struggles for Mastery of the Global Film Industry 1920–1950*, Cambridge, Cambridge University Press.

Vaughan, J. (2002) 'Propaganda by proxy? Britain, America, and Arab Radio Broadcasting, 1953–1957', *Historical Journal of Film, Radio and Television*, vol.22, no.2, pp.157–72.

Volkmer, I. (1999) *News in the Global Sphere: A Study of CNN and its Impact on Global Communication*, Luton, University of Luton Press.

Wagnleitner, R. (1994) *Coca-Colonization and the Cold War: The Cultural Mission of the United States in Austria after World War 2*, Chapel Hill, NC, University of North Carolina Press.

Williams, R. (1966) *Communications* (revised 2nd edn), London, Chatto and Windus.

Wilson, E. (2003) *Media, Meddling and Mediocrity*, Adam Smith Institute Research Paper, www.adamsmith.org/policy/publications/pdf-files/media-meddling.pdf (accessed 7 February 2005).

Wasko, J. (2003) *How Hollywood Works*, London, Sage.

Media organisations and media texts: production, autonomy and power

Chapter 2

David Hesmondhalgh

Contents

1 Introduction

One of the main aims of this book is to examine how media production shapes the everyday words, images and sounds that we see and hear. While in the previous chapter the relationship between media production and media texts was important, but somewhat in the background, here I want to home in on this relationship. Chapter 1 took something of a bird's eye view of large media corporations, but here we swoop closer to look at analysis of what happens inside media organisations, and of how this affects the texts that such organisations produce. In particular, I am concerned here with analysis that has considered how power and inequality in modern societies relate to media organisations. To what extent are media organisations free of powerful interests in modern societies? To what extent do they serve these interests? These questions concern the *autonomy* or independence of media producers.

Let me begin by saying more about the concepts of power and producer autonomy. Power is probably best defined in this context as the ability to exert influence. We need to distinguish between different forms and sites of *social* power. Some institutions and people have great economic power – the ability to mobilise and accrue financial and monetary resources. Others can be said to have political and/or coercive power, such as the ability to direct military forces or police forces. And others can be said to have symbolic or cultural power – the ability to create symbols and meanings which are publicly circulated and which affect people's views of the world. Education, religion and the media are particularly important institutions in this respect. These categories of social power – the economic, the political and the cultural – overlap, and some institutions, such as modern national governments, have significant amounts of all three types of power. One of the reasons that these different forms of social power matter is their relationship to inequality. Modern societies continue to be highly unequal on a number of dimensions, including class, gender and ethnicity (see Braham and Janes, 2002) (see Figure 2.1). These inequalities affect incomes, health, education and life-chances in general (Savage, 2002). If power can be exerted in such a way as to reproduce and even increase such inequalities then this is a serious problem. And, therefore, the relationship of media power to social power matters too. Media which are in thrall to powerful interests, whether consciously or not, have the potential to stifle dissent and reinforce existing inequalities.

There is a long history of debate about the nature and extent of the power *of* the media to shape or contain the range of cultural goods in public circulation, and to affect people's knowledge, values and beliefs. But there is also an important set of debates about how media organisations, with their own particular kinds of power, relate to other

Figure 2.1 *Modern societies continue to be extremely unequal*
Source: Camera Press

forms and sites of power in society. Who, in other words, has power *over* the media? (John Downey addressed these issues when he wrote about debates about media ownership in the previous chapter.) A crucial corollary of this concern with power over the media has been a concern with the degree to which media producers – journalists, musicians, record company personnel, television producers – act *autonomously* of such power. To what degree can media producers create their texts free of the economic, political and cultural preferences of the organisations commissioning and distributing the product?

The issue is not *whether* producers are autonomous *or* dependent on the imperatives of the more powerful groups in society. Conflicts between independence and external control should not be understood as zero-sum games, where, for example, greater constraint by owners and managers automatically leads to less creativity on the part of film-makers, journalists and musicians: in some situations, political or economic constraints can produce probing journalism and innovative entertainment. For this reason, we ought to be suspicious of simple oppositions between control of powerful interests on the one hand and producer autonomy on the other. Nevertheless, analysis of the *tensions* between control and autonomy is an important element of any adequate understanding of the role of the media in modern societies. This chapter, then, explores how different authors have conceived of these tensions. It looks at a number of studies, and compares their understandings of media production, texts and power, and their views of producer autonomy. It also discusses the *methods* used to study these issues.

I begin by looking in Section 2 at how media producers themselves conceive of these issues – which is often that they operate pretty autonomously of powerful interests. I then go on to examine a diametrically opposed view, which argues that media organisations and producers often operate as propagandists for the powerful (Section 3). In Section 4, I examine two studies of crime and the media which see the relationship of media, production and power as somewhat more complex and contested than this, but which nevertheless see the media as reliant on authoritative sources. According to these studies, key media tend to reproduce certain, well-established and powerful viewpoints. In Section 5, I turn to an entertainment genre, rap music, and a study which sees media production as a cultural process. Section 6 examines a study of the BBC in the 1990s which draws attention to the way in which media producers reflect upon their own work and its potential limitations, and which emphasises the agency of such producers. The different studies are summarised in Table 2.1, which appears towards the end of the chapter (and which you can use to help you find your way through these different perspectives).

2   The view from media producers

Let us begin not with academic research but with the views of media workers themselves of the relationships between media production, media texts and power, and between autonomy and control.

Activity 2.1

'The broad shape and nature of the press is ultimately determined by no one but its readers' (former newspaper editor John Whale, quoted in Curran and Seaton, 2003, p.346). Reflect on this quotation for a minute or two. Do you agree with it? ■ ■ ■

John Whale's view is an expression of a position commonly espoused by journalists and other media workers when asked to reflect on the media's role in society. It suggests that media producers simply produce what their audiences demand, because they would go out of business if they did not. There is a strong hint that media producers are therefore not really responsible for what they do. Another view commonly expressed by media producers is that they simply reflect the reality of the world outside the media. Journalists might claim, for example, that they do no more than collate what happens 'out there'. When film-makers or musicians are criticised for providing violent images or sounds, they sometimes respond that they are merely reflecting a violent reality, or distilling the experiences of a particular community of people.

For decades now, sociological examinations of media production processes have aimed to show that the media do not reflect reality or the desires of their audiences, but that they construct pictures of the world based on a variety of different forces. The earliest post-Second World War studies stressed the role of individual 'gatekeepers' in screening and selecting external reality (White, 1950). Later studies emphasised the way in which values, of which media workers were often unconscious, shaped texts. Many journalists would accept this, and few now offer a naively realist view of the relationship between media production, media texts and power.

However, in interviews with media workers, and in reflections of the kind that often appear in newspapers, trade magazines and memoirs, the overwhelming consensus is that media producers operate with high levels of autonomy and independence from the demands of powerful groups in society. Such views are reported not only in public service broadcasting institutions (Schlesinger, 1987) but also from the world of commercial journalism (Weaver and Wilhoit, 1991) and the entertainment industries (Frith, 1983). Such views cannot be dismissed; they are grounded in important facets of media and cultural production in modern societies. There is a long-standing view that art ought to be autonomous of the demands of societies, be they moral, economic or political; and that entertainers should operate on the boundaries of what is felt to be 'normal' or permissible. Journalism too prides itself on its independence from political and economic control. Newspapers may usually be commercial organisations, but a key tenet of journalistic professionalism (see also Chapter 4) is that there should be a clear line between the commercial and the journalistic parts of such organisations. As we shall see, however, the view of many media analysts is that media producers overestimate their autonomy, and instead tend to reproduce viewpoints that, on the whole, support existing patterns of power.

3 Media production as propaganda

Reading 2.1 Activity

Now read the following extract from Edward Herman and Noam Chomsky's book *Manufacturing Consent* (1988). Take notes, and answer the following questions.

- How would you characterise Herman and Chomsky's view of the relationships between the media and powerful groups in society?
- How does this accord with your own view of the media?
- Think of the media coverage of recent foreign conflicts. To what extent does this coverage support their analysis?

Reading 2.1

Edward S. Herman and Noam Chomsky, 'A propaganda model'

The mass media serve as a system for communicating messages and symbols to the general populace. It is their function to amuse, entertain, and inform, and to inculcate individuals with the values, beliefs, and codes of behavior that will integrate them into the institutional structures of the larger society. In a world of concentrated wealth and major conflicts of class interest, to fulfil this role requires systematic propaganda. [...]

In countries where the levers of power are in the hands of a state bureaucracy, the monopolistic control over the media, often supplemented by official censorship, makes it clear that the media serve the ends of a dominant elite. It is much more difficult to see a propaganda system at work where the media are private and formal censorship is absent. This is especially true where the media actively compete, periodically attack and expose corporate and governmental malfeasance, and aggressively portray themselves as spokesmen for free speech and the general community interest. What is not evident (and remains undiscussed in the media) is the limited nature of such critiques, as well as the huge inequality in command of resources, and its effect both on access to a private media system and on its behavior and performance.

A propaganda model focuses on this inequality of wealth and power and its multilevel effects on mass-media interests and choices. It traces the routes by which money and power are able to filter out the news fit to print, marginalize dissent, and allow the government and dominant private interests to get their messages across to the public. The essential ingredients of our propaganda model, or set of news 'filters,' fall under the following headings: (1) the size, concentrated ownership, owner wealth, and profit orientation of the dominant mass-media firms; (2) advertising as the primary income source of the mass media; (3) the reliance of the media on information provided by government, business, and 'experts' funded and approved by these primary sources and agents of power; (4) 'flak' as a means of disciplining the media; and (5) 'anticommunism' as a national religion and control mechanism. These elements interact with and reinforce one another. The raw material of news must pass through successive filters, leaving only the cleansed residue fit to print. They fix the premises of discourse and interpretation, and the definition of what is newsworthy in the first place, and they explain the basis and operations of what amount to propaganda campaigns.

The elite domination of the media and marginalization of dissidents that results from the operation of these filters occurs so naturally that media news people, frequently operating with complete integrity and goodwill, are able to convince themselves that they choose and interpret the news 'objectively' and on the basis of professional news values. Within the limits of the filter constraints they often are objective; the constraints are so powerful, and are built into the system in such a fundamental way, that alternative bases of news choices are hardly imaginable. [...]

The five filters narrow the range of news that passes through the gates, and even more sharply limit what can become 'big news,' subject to sustained news campaigns. By definition, news from primary establishment sources meets one major filter requirement and is readily accommodated by the mass media. Messages from and about dissidents and weak, unorganized individuals and groups, domestic and foreign, are at an initial disadvantage in sourcing costs and credibility, and they often do not comport with the ideology or interests of the gatekeepers and other powerful parties that influence the filtering process. [...]

Thus, for example, the torture of political prisoners and the attack on trade unions in Turkey will be pressed on the media only by human-rights activists and groups that have little political leverage. The U.S. government supported the Turkish martial-law government from its inception in 1980, and the U.S. business community has been warm towards regimes that profess fervent anticommunism, encourage foreign investment, repress unions, and loyally support U.S. foreign policy (a set of virtues that are frequently closely linked). Media that chose to feature Turkish violence against their own citizenry would have had to go to extra expense to find and check out information sources; they would elicit flak from government, business, and organized right-wing flak machines, and they might be looked upon with disfavor by the corporate community (including advertisers) for indulging in such a quixotic interest and crusade. They would tend to stand alone in focusing on victims that from the standpoint of dominant American interests were *unworthy*. [...]

In marked contrast, protest over political prisoners and the violation of the rights of trade unions in Poland was seen by the Reagan administration and business elites in 1981 as a noble cause, and, not coincidentally, as an opportunity to score political points. Many media leaders and syndicated columnists felt the same way. Thus information and strong opinions on human-rights violations in Poland can be obtained from official sources in Washington, and reliance on Polish dissidents would not elicit flak from the U.S. government or the flak machines. These victims would be generally acknowledged by the managers of the filters to be *worthy*.

Reading source

Herman and Chomsky, 1988, pp.1–2, 31–2 ■ ■ ■

Herman and Chomsky take a very negative and sceptical view of the role of the media in modern societies. The term 'propaganda' bluntly and provocatively drives home their interpretation. The term is usually used to refer to very deliberate manipulation of symbols to affect people's opinions and attitudes. In a highly unequal world, Herman and Chomsky see the media as serving the interests of a dominant elite; and, importantly, they claim that this fact is much harder to see in liberal democracies than in dictatorships. So the media are servants of the powerful, but worse still, the system works in such a way that this is obscured, not only for the public, but also for media producers, who often act in good faith, and yet *still* produce news which favours existing structures of inequality and power.

Herman and Chomsky's explanation for this is that what happens in the world is filtered by a series of factors before it becomes news. The extracts you have read only signal their views on these filters, but Herman and Chomsky go on to elaborate. The first filter works in the following way: 'the dominant media firms are large businesses; they are controlled by very wealthy people or by managers who are subject to sharp constraints by owners and other market-profit-oriented forces; and they are closely interlocked, and have important common interests, with other major corporations, banks and government' (Herman and Chomsky, 1988, p.14). These factors, as we have seen in Chapter 1, form a vital aspect of political economy approaches to the media. The second filter, advertising, makes media companies reliant on the decisions of advertisers (this has also been an important theme in media political economy). This allows advertisers to favour culturally and politically conservative programming and to discriminate politically against working-class and radical media. The third filter is that the media save time and money by constantly turning to sources that are considered 'credible' by society as a whole, and this favours the already-established and powerful over the marginalised and powerless. We will return to this point in Section 4. The fourth filter, 'flak', refers to the way in which governments and businesses assail, threaten and 'correct' the media, 'trying to contain any deviations from the established line' (Herman and Chomsky, 1988, p.28). The fifth filter, anticommunism, means that support for measures intended to combat social inequality is deemed dangerous, because of the association of equality with communism. Perhaps Herman and Chomsky would now update this filter, adapting anticommunism to patriotism or, more specifically, anti-Islam, for the era of 'the war against terrorism'.

The examples Herman and Chomsky give in their extract are taken from the 1980s. Their complaint is that the Polish government (an enemy of the US state at the time) and the Turkish government (then, and to a lesser extent now, a friend of the USA) both behaved brutally towards dissidents, but only the brutality of the Polish government was reported in the US news media. You may have heard similar complaints in more recent years about the way in which, for example, the brutality of the Iraqi regime of Saddam Hussein received a great deal of news coverage in the run-up to the Gulf Wars of 1991 and 2003 (see Figure 2.2), but the brutality of governments friendly to the US state, such as Indonesia, where military forces have been involved in mass killings at least as bad as those perpetrated by Iraqi forces, have been much less reported in the Western media. On the other hand, you might not have heard similar complaints; for an important part of Herman and Chomsky's case concerns the way in which large sections of the public never get to hear news that significantly undermines the interests of the powerful.

Herman and Chomsky's views of the relationships between media texts, production and power have been the subject of a great deal of comment. Two British media political economists, Peter Golding and Graham Murdock, have described this model as *instrumentalist*: media companies are seen as instruments or tools of state or class power. While they agree with Herman and Chomsky that governments and business elites have considerable power, Golding and Murdock feel that Herman and Chomsky overstate their case, and that 'the contradictions in the system' are overlooked (Golding and Murdock, 2000, p.73). Herman and Chomsky do acknowledge the existence within the mainstream media of reporting that is critical of existing power structures, but they are very

Enough germs to kill everyone on the planet

DR GERM: Taha looks disturbingly normal for a ghoul

THE EVIL SCIENTIST

This is the British-trained demon of death whose ghoulish experiments with anthrax, botulism and bubonic plague have earned her the nickname Dr Germ.

Her real name is Rihab Taha, she has prepared enough toxic bombs for Iraq's Saddam Hussein to wipe out the world twice over and is a prime target in the West's war against

BY **LEWIS PANTHER**

terrorism.

Nowadays, with the money Saddam heaps on her for each new weapon of mass destruction she devises, Taha favours sharp Armani suits. But staff at Norwich University recall a drab, mousey-haired girl who arrived in 1979 to study for her PhD in biology,

specialising in plant poisons.

Desperate to maintain a low profile she moved into an Edwardian terraced house in the city's Earlham Road.

In 1979 Taha, who was then 23, was already a dedicated member of Saddam's ruling Ba'arth party. Intelligence sources suspect she was sent to Norwich for training after being recruited to Iraq's nuclear, biological and chemical (NBC) warfare programme.

When Taha returned to Iraq she headed straight to one of the country's many military research centres and presented her true life's work, carefully written over long nights in the Earlham Road flat – plans for mass destruction.

She shrewdly married the head of Iraq's weapons programme General Amer Rashid, a man educated in London. Soon she had his baby and whiled away the months of pregnancy researching methods of infecting Western tots

with lethal doses of diarrhoea.

Israeli intelligence agents uncovered evidence of anthrax bomb tests on human guinea pigs at Salman Park, a military complex 50 miles south of Baghdad.

Their reports describe how Iraqi scientists watched from behind a glass screen as Iranian prisoners, captured during the 1980–88 war with Iraq, were strapped to beds.

They were sprayed with anthrax from a ceiling-mounted 'gun' and their agonising deaths exactly timed by Taha's scientists over 48 hours.

On Friday, President Bush gave his clearest hint that Saddam Hussein might be the next target in the war against terrorism.

And tellingly, in a military research paper USAF major Brian Anderson says: "There is only one name ahead of Taha's on the US's list of Middle Eastern enemies ... Saddam Hussein."

Figure 2.2 The run-up to the Iraq War of 2003 saw a great deal of press coverage of the brutality of Saddam Hussein's Iraqi regime and of Iraq's possession of 'weapons of mass destruction'. Might such stories as this, from the UK's biggest-selling Sunday newspaper, The News of the World, confirm Herman and Chomsky's propaganda model?

Source: *The News of the World*, 14 October 2001

quick to dismiss such critical journalism. The media 'periodically attack and expose corporate and governmental malfeasance', say Herman and Chomsky, in Reading 2.1, but they immediately point to 'the limited nature of such critiques'. While they recognise that the media do not consist entirely of outlets supporting the interests of the most powerful, at the same time they portray those who most rigorously oppose these interests as heroic outsiders.

The provision of alternative media outlets is important, but we need also to look at contradictions *within* the 'mainstream' media to understand the relationship between media and power adequately. An example of such contradictions might be, to return to the case of reporting of foreign conflicts, the fact that many news organisations questioned the war in Iraq in 2003. The US media analyst Daniel Hallin has provided a model which potentially allows us to understand such contradictions better than Herman and Chomsky's model – see Figure 2.3. The media will often advocate or promote widely supported views or institutions in times of consensus. Beyond this is a 'sphere of legitimate controversy' (Hallin, 1986, p.117), such as electoral contests and debates over policy. Here journalists will try to maintain objectivity and balance. Beyond this is 'the sphere of deviance', where those deemed to be outside mainstream politics are excluded or condemned. There are gradations within each sphere (consensus, legitimate controversy and deviance) and people, topics and institutions can move between spheres. Hallin, then, usefully deals with questions of contradiction, change and dissent among the powerful. These are issues to which we shall return.

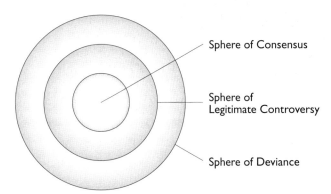

Figure 2.3 *Hallin's model: spheres of consensus, controversy and deviance*
Source: Hallin, 1986, p.117

How do Herman and Chomsky see the autonomy and independence of newsmakers? In Reading 2.1, Herman and Chomsky say that media news people often act with 'complete integrity and goodwill', but still produce output that is skewed in a way that Herman and Chomsky see as a threat to the public good. It seems that most journalists are part of a system of propaganda which they completely fail to recognise, while others 'choose to conform' (Chomsky, quoted by Klaehn, 2002, p.151). As an advocate of the propaganda model puts it, 'meanings are formed and produced at an unconscious level' (Klaehn, 2002, p.150). Edward Herman has quite explicitly stated that questions concerning the intentions of media producers are of no importance in his view: 'The propaganda model explains media behavior and performance in structural terms, and intent is an unmeasurable red herring. All we know is that the media and journalists often mislead in tandem – some no doubt internalise a propaganda line as true, some may know it is false, but the point is unknowable and unimportant' (Herman, 2000, p.105). Yet the term 'propaganda' strongly implies deliberate manipulation – it seems that many media producers, according to this view, are unwitting puppets of powerful interests in society, especially big businesses and the US state.

As we shall see, many who study media production feel that this overstates the case. As John Corner (2003) points out, if the aim of media criticism is to reform and improve media practice, it is hard not to wonder how media producers would respond to being told that they are for the most part full of integrity, but are spending their working lives in a state of delusion. On the other hand, as Corner also points out, it is sometimes necessary to make uncomfortable criticisms in order to bring about reform.

Further controversy surrounds the methods used by Herman and Chomsky to justify their model. According to Chomsky, in another book, (Chomsky, 1989, p.153), the propaganda model makes predictions at various levels. He distinguishes three orders of prediction:

- about how the media function;
- about how media performance will be discussed and evaluated in society;
- about reactions to studies of media performance.

'The general prediction, at each level', says Chomsky, is 'that what enters into the mainstream will support the needs of established power'. The main method used by the propaganda model to test these predictions is 'to consider the spectrum of opinion allowed expression' (Chomsky, 1989, p.59), that is, to investigate media coverage (of their main area of interest – foreign conflicts), and to assess whether it includes opinions which, in their view, would challenge 'established power'. So an important part of their case draws on a particular form of textual analysis known as content analysis (see **Hesmondhalgh, 2006**). As we have seen, the model also presents a series of factors as explanations about *why* producers act in the way that they do – the five filters. But when it comes to explaining coverage in actual cases, the mechanisms by which producers are led to report in a certain way are left out of the picture. The result is that the outline of the model suggests a view of both production and texts, but only the texts are truly examined.

Finally, as with all models, we need to consider how wide a range of instances the model can be used to explain satisfactorily. Herman and Chomsky's book provides a good deal of evidence to show that US reporting of foreign news overwhelmingly supported the interests of the US government. But how far is the idea of propaganda applicable to other areas of news coverage, to news coverage in other societies, and to non-news media output? In their preface to *Manufacturing Consent* (1988), Herman and Chomsky make it clear that 'We do not claim this is all the mass media do, but we believe the propaganda function to be a very important aspect of their overall service' (Herman and Chomsky, 1988, p.xi). But how important? What is the relation of propaganda to other aspects of the media's service? What are these other aspects? We are not told, but Herman and Chomsky often seem to imply strongly that they are describing a very large proportion indeed of the media's role. The opening paragraph of Reading 2.1, which is the first paragraph of the main body of their book, puts enormous emphasis on the way in which the media integrate individuals into the institutional structure of society. In that paragraph, Herman and Chomsky seem to make systematic propaganda the main condition of this integrative role – indeed, perhaps, the only one.

In summary, then, Herman and Chomsky see the media as propagandists for the economically and politically powerful, via the filtering effect of various economic and ideological factors. They focus mainly on news texts, and see the detailed study of media producers and media organisations as more or less irrelevant. And the professional autonomy of journalists is, for them, illusory. In the next section, I will look at two studies, both of which happen to be about crime reporting, which would concur with the view that the media can act in the service of powerful interests in society, but which place much more emphasis on organisational processes and on the *contested* nature of journalism.

4 Contesting crime

Activity 2.2

Take a look at your local newspaper and scan through to see how many stories concern crime; or watch a local news bulletin. Why are there so many stories about crime? ■ ■ ■

Crime is a staple of the media (See Figure 2.4.). It involves events that can dramatically alter the lives of those involved and so is often used for dramatic entertainment, and even titillation. Some journalists would no doubt argue that the widespread coverage of crime (especially in local newspapers and broadcasting) reflects the desires of audiences to read and hear stories of this kind. But news about crime is also often cheap to gather, as journalists can gain information about incidents and court appearances easily and quickly from the police and from courts. The reporting of crime has extremely serious implications for the criminal justice system and for public perceptions of society.

mknews

Wednesday, February 23, 2005   No. 130   **The independent voice of Milton Keynes**   50p where sold

Advertising: 01908 809000   Newsdesk: 01908 809809   Distribution: 0845 2302696 (local call rate)   www.lsnmedia.co.uk

Report shows dramatic increase in drunk and disorderly cases

VIOLENT DRUNKS INFLATE CITY CRIME FIGURES

VIOLENT crime in the city centre is on the increase according to a shock new police report.

Members of Milton Keynes Council licensing committee will hear tonight how the last 12 months has seen a dramatic rise in the numbers of attacks on people.

Figures reveal there were 222 more offences last year than in 2003 – a total of 816 crimes or more than two incidents for every day of the year.

The report, compiled by Supt Simon Blake, also shows that all city centre crime has increased by 12 per cent in 2004 compared to the previous year from 4,362 crimes to 4,881. The city centre now accounts for 17.9 per cent of all crime recorded in Milton Keynes.

It is part of an overall trend of increasing crime in Milton Keynes which has seen 3,370 more cases city-wide.

The number of prosecutions for drunk and disorderly has also seen 'a dramatic increase' from 618 offences last year to 726 for the period between October 2003 and September 2004.

Of those, 20 were under 18 years old.

Supt Blake said: "My officers are reporting that the numbers of persons seemingly drunk are still on the increase.

"I again stress that the licensee has a moral duty in helping to prevent these offences committed by persons who have consumed to excess in premises close to the location of the offences."

The report makes grim reading just months after licensing laws were relaxed to allow 24 hour drinking.

Pubs across the city have been able to apply for 24 hour licences since November and Supt Blake fears the situation could become worse.

"It has been a very busy year," he said.

"Which I feel will only become busier over the next 12 months with the newly proposed Licensing Act."

His words reflect the view of Supt Liam Macdougall who spoke to this paper in November saying: "It will be necessary for police and the licensing authority to co-operate and work responsibly in order to minimise any negative consequences the new act may have and ensure alcohol-related crime does not become a significant problem."

Police are hoping new Government laws giving officers the power to impose fixed penalty spot fines and the information-sharing Milton Keynes Bar Watch scheme will help curb the increase in crime.

craig.lewis@mk-news.co.uk

Hunt defies ban
– pictures page 23

Bypass protesters light candles and read poems for fallen trees

Police and security watch as a tree goes down last week

ANTI-bypass protesters have held a candlelight vigil - in memory of some felled trees.

More than two dozen took part in the vigil on Sunday near to the site of the planned Stoke Hammond/ Linslade bypass.

The vigil comes only days after High Court officers backed by scores of police and security staff reclaimed the land occupied by activists.

Many protesters had been living in tree houses and tents preventing building work on the new road beginning.

Last Tuesday Bucks County Council used an injunction and possession order to have protestors evicted. The contractors moved in and several mature trees

including a 150-year-old oak were felled.

But the activists have vowed to battle on.

It's Stop The Linslade Bypass website says the vigil was held 'in memory of the trees' which had been 'murdered' to make way for the road and was an attempt to 'show the council that we are still here and still care'.

As well as lighting candles, people read poems and said prayers in what was described as a 'short and very moving ceremony'.

A Bucks county council spokesman said: "The work is still going ahead and the workmen are still clearing the site as they are aiming to get on schedule. We are also maintaining security levels."

THIS WEEK: Nineteen pages of motor ads starts page 59 Check out our NEW CAR feature on page 71

Figure 2.4 *Stories on crime are a staple of local newspapers. They are dramatic and easy to obtain but they may add to fears of crime*

4.1 News sources as primary definers

In 1978 a group of researchers at the Centre for Contemporary Cultural Studies at the University of Birmingham (Stuart Hall, Chas Critcher, Tony Jefferson, John Clarke and Brian Roberts) published *Policing the Crisis: Mugging, the State, and Law and Order* (Hall et al., 1978), a long and detailed analysis of how media coverage of crime in the early 1970s reflected and helped to create a sense of crisis in British society at that time. Their stance was explicitly Marxist, and more specifically it was influenced by the Italian politician Antonio Gramsci (1891–1937) (see Figure 2.5) and his concept of 'hegemony'. This refers to the domination, by a class 'bloc' or coalition, over subordinate groups; but the most important feature of Gramsci's writings on hegemony for the Birmingham cultural studies researchers was the idea that hegemony was achieved not necessarily through coercion, but primarily through the winning of *consent* by 'moral and intellectual leadership'. Stuart Hall and his colleagues updated Gramsci's theories (combining them with others, such as theories of youth deviance, and of the importance of language) to try to understand how 'an authoritarian consensus' emerged in the 1970s, a 'conservative backlash' against the more liberal and tolerant cultural values which had developed in the 1950s and 1960s. They examined how the fears and anxieties behind media reporting of mugging, and the public response to it, resonated with long-standing attitudes to social change, and more broadly, with a contemporary 'crisis of hegemony' in the British state.

This context is very important but what concerns us most here is the book's view of the relationship between media texts, media production and power. Hall et al. examined a spate of stories in the British national press about 'mugging', a supposedly new strain of crime involving violent robbery, which appeared between August 1972 and September 1973 (see Figure 2.6). They showed that in fact neither the crime nor the label were new: it was almost impossible to glean from official statistics whether such robberies were on the increase, and the term itself came from the United States, where it was particularly associated with the reporting of robberies carried out by young African-American men. Hall et al. showed convincingly that the widespread use of the term was driven by a particular set of anxieties about 'race', crime and youth. Mugging became the basis of a moral panic, defined by another sociologist as a situation in which 'a condition, episode, person or group of persons emerges to become defined as a threat to societal values and interests' (Stan Cohen, quoted by Hall et al., p.16). The response from the police was

Figure 2.5 *Antonio Gramsci (1891–1937)*
Source: International Gramsci Society

to put together an 'anti-mugging campaign' which resulted in a number of arrests – and in some prominent cases, abandoned trials – of young black men. The response from the judiciary was a drastic increase in sentences.

Hall et al. attempted to explain 'the "fit" between dominant ideas and professional media ideologies and practices' (Hall et al., 1978, p.57). They did so in a way somewhat different from Herman and Chomsky's later

Figure 2.6 *One of a number of stories about mugging which appeared in the UK press in the early 1970s (see Reading 2.2)*
Source: *Daily Mirror*, 15 August 1972

approach. This fit was not, said Hall et al., because of ownership (which, as we have seen, Herman and Chomsky emphasise) for, in their view, journalists have 'day-to-day "relative autonomy" [...] from economic control' (Hall et al., 1978, p.57). Rather, it was because of two factors: certain news values held by journalists, and the routine structures of news production. News values are the criteria by which journalists select which items to feature and privilege (Hall et al. used an influential study on news values by Galtung and Ruge, 1965). Stories that are unexpected and dramatic, and which involve negative consequences (especially human tragedy) and elite persons, for example, will tend to be favoured over stories that do not have these attributes (Hall et al., 1978, p.54). For Hall et al., routine is even more important than news values in explaining the 'fit' between dominant ideas and professional practice (p.58). Drawing on a number of studies emphasising the importance of such routine, Hall et al. claimed that 'The media do not themselves autonomously create news items; rather they are "cued in" to specific new topics by regular and reliable institutional sources' (p.57). This was partly because of the pressure of time in making the news, and partly because journalism is supposed to operate with some degree of objectivity. Together, these factors meant that journalists constantly turned to 'accredited representatives of major social institutions' (p.58). The result of this structured preference was that these accredited representatives of powerful institutions become the *primary definers* of topics, such as crime; the media are merely the *secondary definers*. This permits the primary definers to establish the initial definition, or *primary interpretation*, of any topic (p.58).

So how does this apply to crime news in general and to mugging in particular?

Reading 2.2 Activity

Read the following extract from *Policing the Crisis* (1978). Hall et al. firstly elaborate on their model of primary and secondary definers in relation to crime reporting; then they apply the model to what they call the 'reciprocal relations' between the primary definers and the media. As you read, think about recent crime reporting. Have any other 'scares' been used to justify police and judicial crackdowns?

Stuart Hall, Chas Critcher, Tony Jefferson, John Clarke and Brian Roberts, 'The social production of news'

We saw previously how the production of news is dependent on the role played by primary definers. In the area of crime news, the media appear to be more heavily dependent on the institutions of crime control for their news stories than in practically any other area. The police, Home Office spokesmen and the courts form a near-monopoly as sources of crime news in the media. Many professional groups have contact with crime, but it is only the police who claim a *professional* expertise in the 'war against crime', based on daily, *personal* experience. This exclusive and particular 'double expertise' seems to give police spokesmen especially authoritative credence. In addition, both the formal and informal social relations of news-making from which the journalist derives his [*sic*] 'crime' material are dependent on a notion of 'trust', e.g. between the police and the crime correspondent; i.e. on reliable and objective reporting by the journalist of the privileged information to which he is allowed access. A 'betrayal' of that trust will lead to the drying up of the flow of information. [...] The Home Office, which is invested with the ultimate political and administrative responsibility for crime control, is accredited because of its responsibility to Parliament and hence, ultimately, to the 'will of the people'. The special status of the courts we have noted earlier. Judges have the responsibility for disposing of the transgressors of society's legal code; this inevitably gives them authority. But the constant media attention to their weighty pronunciations underlines the importance of their *symbolic* role: their status as representatives and 'ventriloquists' for the good and the upright against the forces of evil and darkness. What is most striking about crime news is that it very rarely involves a first-hand account of the crime itself, unlike the 'eye-witness' report from the battlefront of the war correspondent. Crime stories are almost wholly produced from the definitions and perspectives of the institutional primary definers.

This near-monopoly situation provides the basis for the *three* typical formats for crime news which together cover most variants of crime stories. First, the report based on police statements about investigations of a particular case – which involve a police reconstruction of the event and details of the action they are taking. Second, the 'state of the war against crime report' – normally based on Chief Constables' or Home Office statistics about current crime, together with an interpretation by the spokesmen of what the bare figures mean – what is the most serious challenge, where there has been most police success, etc. Third, the staple diet of crime reporting – the story based on a court case: some, where the case is held to be especially newsworthy, following the day-to-day events of the trial; others where just the day of sentencing, and especially the judge's remarks, are deemed newsworthy; and still others which consist merely of brief summary reports.

[...]

[W]e want to look at the *relations of reciprocity* between the primary definers and the media, as exemplified in the mugging case. On 26 September 1972 the *Daily Mirror* carried a story with the headline 'A Judge Cracks Down On Muggers In City Of Fear.' The story perfectly illustrates the role and status for the media of privileged definitions: the use of the term 'muggers' in the headline is justified by the judge's statement in the main report: 'Mugging is becoming more and more prevalent certainly in London. We are told that in America people are afraid to walk the streets late at night because of mugging.' We must also take note here of the judge's use of American 'mugging' as a reference point against which his sentencing is contextualised; but primarily this example illustrates the 'anchorage' of news-stories in the authoritative pronouncements of privileged definers *outside* the media.

In October 1972, we find an example of how the media utilises a 'base' in such definitions for its *own* definitional work on such an issue. The *Daily Mirror* on 6 October 1972 accompanied a report of Judge Hines's sentencing three teenage youths to three years' imprisonment for 'mugging' with an editorial which picked up his statement that 'The course I feel I am bound to take may not be the best for you young men individually, but it is one I must take in the public interest.' The editorial *adds its own campaigning 'voice'* – its 'public idiom' – to that of the judge: 'Judge Hines is right. There are times when deterrent sentences which normally would seem harsh and unfair, MUST be imposed ... if mugging is not to get out of hand as it has in America, punishment must be sharp and certain.' Here we can see the press in a more active role – justifying (but simultaneously using as its justification) judicial statements about 'mugging' as a public issue. The circle has become tighter, the topic more closed, the relations between media and primary definers more mutually reinforcing. (Indeed for the *Mirror there is no debate left*: 'Judge Hines is right.')

Reading source

Hall et al., 1978, pp.68–9, 74–5 ■ ■ ■

As I write, the most prominent recent example that comes to mind of a scare being used to justify a crime 'crackdown', in the way Hall et al. describe with 'mugging', is recent coverage of sexual offences against children (often labelled 'paedophilia' stories. See Figure 2.7). But more generally, in the UK, there is a continuing competition between political parties to be 'tough on crime'. And in the USA, the longstanding crackdown on crime has helped lead to what one commentator has called a 'carceral society': in 1975, US prisons had 380,000 inmates; by 2000, this figure had risen to over two million, 'even as crime levels remained stagnant' (Wacquant, 2002, p.50). The lifelong cumulative probability of going to prison, based on the imprisonment rates of the early 1990s, was 4 per cent for whites and 29 per cent for African-Americans (Wacquant, 2002, p.43). So Hall et al.'s concerns about crime, 'race' and the media continue to be extremely topical, but how might we assess their explanation of media production?

Hall et al. see the relationships between media texts, media production and power as more complex than Herman and Chomsky do. This is partly because they have a different conception of ideological conflict and power, based on Gramsci's emphasis on the troubled process of the winning of consent. However, their view of media production itself is somewhat similar to that of Herman and Chomsky: the media are in essence unwitting servants of the powerful. In this respect, then, their view of the autonomy and independence of journalists comes close to that of the propaganda model. In terms of method, like Herman and Chomsky, Hall et al. rely on readings of media texts, and on assumptions about media production processes, to construct their views. And in terms of range, like Herman and Chomsky, they make relatively little effort to say how generalisable their model is to other forms of media coverage. However, this is perhaps less of a fault in the case of Hall et al.'s *Policing the Crisis* than in Herman and Chomsky's *Manufacturing Consent*, given that Hall et al.'s treatment of media production is only one part of an attempt to understand British culture and ideology in the 1970s through the prism of 'mugging'.

4.2 Competing sources

Two British sociologists, Philip Schlesinger and Howard Tumber, have made a number of criticisms of Hall et al.'s view of the relations between news sources and news media. The following are the most relevant for our present purposes (here I summarise Schlesinger and Tumber, 1994, pp.17–21).

Figure 2.7 *The UK press in the 2000s has featured many stories about 'paedophiles'. These are often linked to calls for restrictions on civil liberties in the name of protecting children*

1 The concept of primary definition is problematic. Official sources sometimes compete with each other in trying to influence the construction of a story. In such a situation, who is the primary definer?

2 There are huge inequalities of access to the media among the privileged, and Hall et al. fail to consider this factor. Prime ministers and presidents have much greater access than most other politicians, for example.

3 There is nothing in Hall et al.'s model of media as secondary definers, and powerful sources as primary definers, which addresses the question of changes over time in access to the news media. How do sources become less powerful and more powerful over time?

4 The notion of the media as secondary definers overstates the passivity of the media. Sometimes the media challenge the so-called primary definers. Prominent examples include the BBC *Today* programme's challenge to the British government's 'evidence' that Saddam Hussein's Iraq had ready-to-use weapons of mass destruction in the build-up to the Gulf War of 2003. Indeed, such challenges are a vital part of how many journalists conceive of their work (you may recall that Herman and Chomsky were explicitly dismissive of such challenges; Hall et al. are dismissive too, but implicitly).

5 Hall et al.'s model homogenises the media. Some media outlets allow much greater access to alternative sources than others.

6 The conception of primary definition 'renders largely invisible the activities of sources that attempt to generate "counter-definitions". This rules out any analysis of the process of negotiation about policy questions between power holders and their opponents that may occur prior to the issuing of what are assumed to be primary definitions' (Schlesinger and Tumber, 1994, p.21).

Schlesinger and Tumber are *not* questioning the view that journalism generally favours the views and interests of authoritative sources, but they are keen to draw attention to 'the dynamic processes of contestation in a given field of discourse' (Schlesinger and Tumber, 1994, p.21) which, in their view, Hall et al. downplay. They portray a complex world of multiple, competing sources, struggling to affect the media and policy agendas about crime. Professional associations such as the Police Federation and the Prison Officers Association employ sophisticated techniques to promote the interests of their members to the media, especially when it comes to trying to form and shape crime policy. These groups are often competing with pressure groups, such as Liberty (formerly the National Council for Civil Liberties) and NACRO (the National Association for the Care and Resettlement of Offenders).

All these organisations have paid great attention to developing sophisticated ways of gaining the sustained attention of the media, and this adds to the battle to define crime.

How does Schlesinger and Tumber's conception of media production, media texts and power compare to those of Hall et al. and Herman and Chomsky? Like Hall et al., and like many other empirical studies of journalism (see, for example, Ericson et al., 1989), Schlesinger and Tumber are particularly concerned with the relationships between media and sources as a way of understanding media production. Much more than Hall et al. and Herman and Chomsky, though, Schlesinger and Tumber portray media production as a *contested* field. A key influence is the work of the French sociologist Pierre Bourdieu (Schlesinger makes this clear elsewhere; see Schlesinger, 1990, p.779) (see Figure 2.8). Bourdieu wrote only briefly and problematically about the media, but his work provides detailed studies of how different, competing groups struggle for positions of power and influence in various 'fields', such as literature, art, education and taste (see, for example, Bourdieu ,1996). Bourdieu stresses how the less prestigious and accredited can also achieve influence, through positioning themselves as pure outsiders, unsullied by power. This complicates notions of power, showing that power does not operate exclusively in a top-down way, but involves complex dynamics and forms. Schlesinger and Tumber would claim that this helps them to produce a more nuanced and more complex picture of media production than Hall et al. (It also reflects a shift in leftist sociology, and in media studies, away from the influence of Marxism in the late 1980s and 1990s.)

Methodologically, Schlesinger and Tumber take a very different route from Herman and Chomsky and Hall et al. Instead of reading off production processes from media texts, they conducted interviews with media producers about their working lives, and also with sources, the people from whom journalists get their information. Many studies already existed that were based on interviews with, and observations of, journalists. Schlesinger and Tumber helped to launch a much greater concern with the wider contexts of news production, away from the 'media-centrism' of earlier studies.

What of autonomy and control? The implications of Schlesinger and Tumber's study, and of their approach, are that journalists have some room to negotiate within the brief defined by the particular medium and outlet (newspaper, television programme, etc.) they work for, and can set different sources against each other. But they also suggest that sources have become much more astute and professional in how they work with the media. This could be seen as reducing the autonomy of journalists further, but it also means that campaigning organisations representing the less powerful might have more of an influence than they once did. In this

Figure 2.8 *Pierre Bourdieu (1930–2002)*
Source: Romy de la Mauviniere/AP Photo

respect, then, it may be that Hall et al., who downplay this role for
'alternative' sources, were writing before an era when 'non-official' sources
began to target the media, using professional public relations techniques.
In other words, Hall et al.'s research may have reflected the media–source
relations of a different historical period. But the main point is that, for
Schlesinger and Tumber, journalists are more independent than is implied
by Herman and Chomsky, and by Hall et al., but given that they rarely
depart from a set of conventions, and from particular routines of
working, they are much less autonomous than journalists themselves
would claim.

5 Media production as cultural process: a case study of rap

Like Herman and Chomsky, and Hall and his collaborators, Schlesinger
and Tumber focus strongly on the news, and on how news reporting
might favour existing patterns of power. But what of entertainment?
Here, the links between power and the media might seem more remote,
in that the news reports upon (or ignores) important events in the world.

But entertainment also acts as an important way in which values and beliefs are understood in society, and therefore has implications for understanding the relationships between social power and media power. So let us now look at a study of the production of rap or hip hop, to see how this compares with the approaches to news we have examined so far.

In his book *Music Genres and Corporate Cultures* the British writer Keith Negus declares that he is interested in two processes: an 'industry produces culture' process and 'culture produces an industry' process (Negus, 1999, p.14; see also du Gay, 1997). The first idea refers to the setting up, by companies, of organisational structures and working practices in order to make cultural goods (that is, symbolic goods). For Negus, this process is emphasised by political economy and by the sociological study of organisational structures. The second idea is that production takes place 'in relation to broader culture formations and practices that are within neither the control nor the understanding of the company' (Negus, 1999, p.19). This idea draws on cultural studies and its analysis of the importance of culture as an active element in society, rather than as the by-product of other processes, such as production for profit. For Negus, following cultural studies approaches, culture 'needs to be understood as the *constitutive context* within and out of which the sounds, words and images of popular music are made and given meaning' (Negus, 1999, p.19). Negus's dual emphasis on production of culture and cultures of production is, then, an attempt to reconcile tensions between political economy and cultural studies in the analysis of media production.

What does Negus mean by 'broader culture formations'? This becomes clearer later in his book when he criticises accounts in management studies which study (and sometimes attempt to help create) 'corporate cultures' within organisations. The cultural context within which a company works, says Negus, can have a greater impact on the workings of a corporation than attempts to create a distinctive ethos or culture within an organisation. This raises wider questions about culture: 'to what extent are music industry practices shaped by ... regional, ethnic, religious or linguistic affiliation? How does gender, sexuality or class create patterns which shape the presentation of artists?' (Negus, 1999, p.82). Let us now look at how Negus puts these ideas into practice.

Reading 2.3 Activity

Now read the following extract on 'the business of rap', from an article by Negus, in the context of the above remarks on how Negus contextualises his approach to media production. As you read, consider the following questions.

- In what way, according to Negus, do outside cultural forces affect what happens in the music industry?
- What kinds of effect does this have on media texts, in terms of the status and presence of rap in the USA and internationally?

Reading 2.3

Keith Negus, 'The business of rap'

[R]ap is located within the major companies' rhythm and blues or black music section. Major companies began introducing divisions to deal specifically with black music during the early 1970s. [...]

[T]hese divisions have provided a space for black staff who may not otherwise have gained employment in the industry. In addition, it has ensured that musicians are managed by personnel with knowledge, skills and understanding of r'n'b music. However, the black divisions have often experienced an unstable and uncertain existence. One of the most significant disadvantages is that the department can easily be cut back, closed down or restructured by the corporation. [...]

For as long as they have been in existence the variously named r'n'b/black/urban divisions have been closed down and reopened as a way of dealing with financial booms and slumps, and staffed and re-staffed as senior management has continually changed thinking about how to deal with r'n'b.

This instability intersects with a broader issue of historical continuity. One conspicuous point here is that there are very few senior black executives within the corporate hierarchy who are above the black division and hence involved in the decision about closing down business units or re-staffing existing departments. As Reebee Garofolo has also noted 'black personnel have been systematically excluded from positions of power within the industry' (1994: 275). Hence, the black divisions have not been allowed to develop a continuity and a sense of history that is consonant with the African-American contribution to US musical culture.

It is within this context that the music industry began dealing with rap (or not dealing with rap) during the 1980s. At one point it seemed that the major companies had neither the inclination, understanding nor skills to deal with rap. It was partly anxiety, lack of expertise and incomprehension on the part of the majors which allowed small companies to carve out a considerable niche during the 1980s. [...]

The genre culture of rap posits a different notion of musical practice (not only in the well-documented use of existing musical elements and technologies), but in terms of the idea of a 'career' and sense of belonging to a musical entity. This is quite a contrast from that of the stable, bounded and predictable rock unit or pop band, the solo performer and self-sufficient singer-songwriter which the industry has become competent at producing and comfortable in dealing with. Rap posits a fluid series of affiliations and associations, alliances and rivalries, occasionally serious, and usually related to neighbourhood and representation. These affiliations are lived across various group and individual identities.

This is connected to another issue which the industry has also been uncomfortable with: the representation of 'the real' or what is often referred to as 'being real' and the politics of identity which has accompanied this. This aspect has often received more superficial media coverage than serious debate about the issues which it raises and has frequently been reduced to simple arguments about profanity and the generic imagery of violence and misogyny that has characterized so-called gangsta rap. And 'discussion' is often informed by a simple stimulus–response model of media effects and an aesthetic reductionism through which rap becomes merely lyrics. One consequence, however, is that overt political pressures have been exerted on record companies, from community organizations, government and state forces. This has further encouraged the companies to distance themselves from the genre culture of rap.

Additional judgements made by staff within business affairs and international departments have also had a decisive influence on the acquisition and drawing up of contracts for rap artists. There are two 'business decisions' here which are far more than straightforward commercial judgements. First is an assessment of the ongoing revenue that can be generated from rap; what is referred to as 'catalogue value'. Rap tracks are routinely compared to conventional songs and it is asserted that they cannot be 'covered' – re-recorded, re-sung, re-performed by other artists. Hence, rap tracks are judged to have a short catalogue shelf life, in terms of their ability to bring in ongoing copyright revenue from their re-use. In addition, the rights revenue that rap can generate during any assumed 'shelf life' is considered to be less than other types of music. In the words of one corporate attorney:

> Music publishing and rap is a nightmare because so much of it is parts of songs. You know they have like one eighth of this song and two-thirds of another song. [...] [1]

[...] Hence, less will be paid to artists as advances and royalties, because it is believed that less can be earned.

A further pragmatic business judgement which affects the amount invested in rap is the assumption that it does not 'travel well'. One senior executive in an international department remarked that he had sat in meetings and heard rap recordings being referred to as 'too black' for international promotion [2], a broad sweeping claim that is justified specifically with the assertion that lyrically rap is 'parochial' – although the history of popular music is littered with parochial lyrics appearing in numerous places around the world. [...]

Hence, there are a number of ways in which the music industry seeks to contain rap within a narrow structure of expectations: through confinement within a black division, through arm's-length deals which avoid having to deal with various alliances and affiliations; through judgements about rap's long-term historical and geographical potential to endure. One consequence is straightforward lack of investment, and practices to keep investment down (it is easier to deal with production units than to invest in staff and office space within the company). At the same time, rather than bringing the culture – the people, the practices – into the industry, the companies have tended to maintain a sharp border. This can be contrasted with the treatment of rock in the late 1960s and early 1970s. [...] This has continued, with a new wave of young white males recruited into the US music industry in the early 1990s following the success of Nirvana and the stabilization of grunge into modern or alternative rock.

Rap personnel have not been embraced in the same way. [...] Despite the influence of rap and hip hop on the aesthetics of music, video, fashion, dancing and advertising, the potential of this broader cultural formation to make a direct contribution to day-to-day music industry business practices is not encouraged.

Notes

1   Personal interview, Paul Robinson, Associate General Counsel, Warner Music Group, New York City, 13 February 1996.
2   This was [...] an off-the-record interview.

Reference

Garofalo, R. (1994) 'Culture versus commerce: the marketing of black popular music', *Public Culture*, vol.7, no.1, pp.275–88.

Reading Source

Negus, 1998, pp.369–72   ■ ■ ■

Negus is examining the means by which ethnic inequality in society, including a whole set of assumptions about the status of African-American music (and therefore about African-American culture), feeds into ethnic inequality in the music industry. The music corporations, Negus shows, keep black musical culture separate, at a distance. There is an uncomfortable sense of ghettoisation, with white executives putting a lot of ground between themselves and musicians who make a lot of money for them, but who generate great controversy. One result of all this, emphasised by Negus, is that distinctive production practices – extended networks and communities of friendship and creative collaboration, for example – are not brought into the corporate music industry itself.

What are the effects of these processes on media texts? One direct result briefly mentioned by Negus is that rap may be under-promoted internationally, because of ethnically inflected assessments of its worth. But there is also a strong sense that rock – which Negus sees as a more conservative and predictable form than rap – is given preferential treatment. How then do we reconcile the fact, which Negus himself mentions towards the end of the reading here, that rap and hip hop have had an enormous influence on contemporary popular culture, with the claims that rap and hip hop have been marginalised in the large music corporations? Negus implies that smaller, independent record companies have had to fill the gaps left by the corporations, and while Negus does not make this point, it may be that these smaller record companies do not have the resources to provide funding which might help rap to thrive as a musical form. Rap, the implication seems to be, has to fend for itself.

So Negus offers an intriguing and informative picture of the relationship between media production and power. The concept of culture is absolutely central to the way he theorises this relationship. However, culture is a term with many meanings, and as we saw earlier, Negus is defining it in the broadest possible sense, as the constitutive context for popular music. It is not always clear why Negus prefers culture over other terms, such as society, or the social, or sociocultural processes, or simply context. For example, when Negus asks the important question, 'how does gender, sexuality or class create patterns which shape the presentation of artists?' (Negus, 1999, p.82), are we dealing here with 'culture' or with forms of social identity which are in turn shaped by a variety of processes, including the cultural, but also including an economic and political system where inequality in power is acute? Culture seems to mean everything that is not popular music itself.

Another related problem with Negus's conception of the relations between media production, texts and society stems from the fact that effects on texts are relatively unexplored; in fact, Negus's focus seems to drift towards the working conditions of media producers – the insecurity, vulnerability and marginalisation of black staff – rather than media texts. These working conditions are important (see Chapter 4) but the lack of address of texts reveals an ambiguity in Negus's formulation 'industry produces a culture'. Is the culture produced by this media industry the working 'culture' of media producers, the shared environments and understandings they operate within? Or is it the cultural goods, the texts, produced by companies? Negus identifies the phrase 'industry produces a culture' with the concerns of political economy approaches (see Chapter 1), and political economy tends to be concerned primarily with 'the production of meaning as the exercise of power' (Golding and Murdock, 2000, p.77), so this strongly implies that this part of Negus's formulation concerns how a study of the 'culture' within which media organisations work can help to cast light on the texts produced. Yet beyond the status of rap (which is very ambiguous anyway) Negus has little to say about this. The result is that Negus is actually much stronger in dealing with 'culture produces an industry' than with 'industry produces culture'.

How then can we summarise Negus's view of the relationship of media producers to power? Cultural studies is often assumed to have a relatively optimistic view of the relationship between media and society, at least compared with the supposed pessimism of political economy. In fact, though, Negus's cultural studies approach sees media producers as very much lacking in autonomy from wider social processes. His work is useful in showing, via interviews with media professionals, how what happens in media organisations does not simply reflect social values outside those organisations; instead organisations take their own particular (cultural) forms.

6 Media producers as reflexive and ambivalent: a case study of the BBC

At this point, you might be thinking that pretty much all studies of media production are pessimistic in that they see the autonomy of media producers as very limited. For a different view, and one that combines the study of news and entertainment, I want to turn to a study of the BBC by the British cultural anthropologist Georgina Born. This will also allow us to spotlight a different method for studying media production, that of ethnography. This is an anthropological and sociological method involving the direct observation of members of a particular social group over an extended period of time (see also **Gillespie, 2005** for discussion of the use of this term in studies of audiences). The researcher then outlines, explains and evaluates what s/he has observed. Some important studies of media organisations have used this method, but they have been relatively few, because many media producers are reluctant to allow researchers access over a long enough period to gain the in-depth knowledge necessary to inform an ethnographic account. As with interviews – which many ethnographic studies also use, in addition to direct observation – there are problems in knowing to what extent the situation being observed is affected by the presence of the researcher. But ethnography can provide powerful insight into what happens in media organisations by observing the actions and attitudes of media workers as they go about their everyday business.

Born carried out her ethnographic fieldwork in the current affairs, documentary and drama departments of the BBC between 1996 and 1998 (she also returned in 2001 for some supplementary fieldwork). This was a period of great upheaval in the BBC. Like many other public sector organisations, it was heavily criticised during the 1980s and early 1990s, for being 'unaccountable, inefficient, incompetent, self-serving and secretive' (Born, 2002, p.69). Much of this criticism came from newspapers that were part of media conglomerates whose owners felt that the BBC was taking valuable market share in the radio and television markets where they were keen to be involved. The introduction of market principles into the public sector was felt by the Conservative government of the time, and by many other bodies (such as management consultancies) to be a way of improving performance. John Birt, the Director General of the BBC from 1993 to 2000, 'championed policies focused on accountability and auditing, the pursuit of markets, efficiency drives and the stoking of competition processes' (p.70) as a way of responding to these pressures. Born shows that by the late 1990s there was 'a dense, continuous, overlapping and cyclical series of auditing processes operating at every level of the Corporation' (p.77) – Programme Strategy Reviews, Annual Performance Reviews, etc. She also shows how such auditing was deeply resented within the BBC. For example, attending a meeting of the BBC Drama Group to discuss the 1995–6 Annual Performance Review, she describes how, as people took in the report's use of smiley faces in the draft Review to illustrate the bullet-pointed lists of positive achievements, 'the room collapse[d] in powerless mirth' (p.79).

But Born also shows that the managerial culture of audit existed in parallel with a 'counter-discourse' of 'serving the public, universality, justifying the licence fee, and quality and integrity of output' (p.81). These were 'traditional' BBC values, first formulated by the BBC's first Director General, John Reith, in the 1920s, but Born observed the critical reinvention of these categories for the 1990s.

Born uses the term 'reflexivity', drawn from some of the key debates in social theory of the 1990s, to understand these processes. Reflexivity is 'the phenomenon of increased and increasingly systematized self-monitoring and self-reflection that is held to be characteristic of the modern era' (p.67). But Born distances herself from characterisations of reflexivity by social theorists (most notably Anthony Giddens, Giddens, 1990) which tend to see the phenomenon in mainly positive terms. Instead she distinguishes between, on the one hand, what she calls the institutionalised reflexivity represented by the audit and accountability mechanisms, and, on the other, the 'critical, reflexive counter-discourse' (p.82).

What form did this counter-discourse take in the BBC of the 1990s? Born analyses various interviews she carried out with BBC senior managers and programme makers. She also provides an interesting extract from her diary of observations from her fieldwork.

Reading 2.4 Activity

Now read the following extract from Georgina Born's March 1997 fieldwork diary.

- What is your reaction to this diary?
- To what extent do the *Newsnight* staff seem to you to be fulfilling the Reithian mission of 'serving the public'?

Reading 2.4

Georgina Born, 'Reflexivity and ambivalence: culture, creativity and government in the BBC'

In the weeks leading up the 1997 General Election I am watching some *Newsnight*[1] producers prepare the lead item on poverty in Britain for that evening's program. The idea originates in the 10.30 a.m. editorial meeting: 'What about this new C. of E. poverty initiative? Neither of the f—g parties do anything about poverty – Labour totally ignore it now.' Jeremy Paxman[2] says the figures show that 30 per cent of Britons are currently living in poverty equal to or greater than the poverty indices from any time this century. He suggests interviews with poor people speaking about their experience. Someone else chips in, 'You want something on how the two political traditions that used to care about poverty – one-nation Tory paternalism and Labour radicalism – are both in decline'. There's discussion of going to a city outside London to film poverty: Sheffield? Darlington? Liverpool? Collectively, they try out various angles. The meeting ends: poverty will be the main story. A producer and reporter are dispatched to Coventry to film. The day editor and three others are 'casting' a discussion on poverty. The first idea is to use representatives from the three parties. There is great reluctance; it will be mortally boring. Or, to use an ex-Labour MP, a Militant sympathizer, now a member of Scargill's party, who is involved in direct action on poverty? He's known to be passionate, lively. They plan the graphics: 'Serious stuff, with plenty of hard figures to bring edge and facticity', while the film will be 'fly-on-the-wall-ish'. They laugh a little at the crudity of having film of kids with rickets or TB. The angle is decided: 'The politicians on both sides have forgotten the poor' and the aim is to pin them down.

A couple of hours in: the day editor asks the poverty team how the discussion is going. A producer replies they've activated all their networks, but the problem is that organizations working with the poor tend to be very suspicious of the media. By 4 p.m., the view is that they will have the three politicians and two others: a senior churchman involved in the Church pressure group on poverty, who will chastize the parties for their inaction, and a representative of the poor, preferably a woman to balance the genders.

5.10 p.m. The poverty team still hasn't managed to come up with a '30 per-center', as they call the representative of the poor, to come on tonight's program. Nervously, they joke about finding a '45 per-center' instead, a woman who's articulate and sympathetic but comes from middle England. I ask what the problem is finding someone poor. One replies, 'It's always extremely difficult to get hold of a member of the deprived classes – they're often extremely reluctant to speak to the media'. Another jokes, 'They're so deprived they can't string two sentences together!' He continues, aghast, that in the country he comes from, 'They simply abolished the welfare state at one stroke!' to which a producer who seems to be *Newsnight*'s token right-winger adds *sotto voce*, 'Only way to do it'. I suggest they try a group representing the unemployed. Tom says, 'The Claimants' Union! That's an idea'. He explains what the CU is to a team member who has never heard of it. She is unenthusiastic.

6 p.m. Time is getting short. The program is on air at 10.30 p.m., and they still haven't found a poor person to appear. Now they're down to trying personal contacts and friends.

7 p.m. At last, haphazardly, Tania has found a woman for the 'disco'. She's a divorced, disabled single-parent mother of four who says she knows all about living near the breadline. On the phone to her, Tania gushes, 'Oh, I wish you'd come on the program and say all this. Someone needs to! Jeremy Paxman is lovely, he'll be gentle with you. We'll send a car to collect you and you'll get £50 for coming along'. The woman agrees. Paxman comes out of his room; the producers say 'We've found you a wonderful woman for the poverty debate'. Paxman, with heavy irony: 'Oh great! Is she disabled,

with a snotty child with running sores?' Tania, ignoring the irony: 'Yes, she's in a wheelchair, very articulate – sounds rather middle class actually. And she's bringing along a child for us to look after – can't afford the childcare!' They all rather smirk as it's so perfectly to formula – which is how they seem to experience the process, as 'cast' according to their needs for the debate. They continue with a heavily ambiguous and self-parodic banter: 'We've had a poor person on before, haven't we?' 'Are you sure we haven't had this woman before? She sounds vaguely familiar ...'

Notes

1 *Newsnight* is BBC television's leading late-night news and analysis program, screened each weekday.
2 Jeremy Paxman, one of *Newsnight*'s three core presenters, is probably Britain's best-known serious television journalist, notorious for his aggressive interviews with politicians of all parties.

Reading source

Born, 2002, pp.65–6 ■ ■ ■

My own reaction to this diary extract was mixed. In some respects, there is clear evidence here of how television journalists working in the most prestigious areas of the media are completely cut off from the lives of working-class British people. Their frantic efforts to find one person from the poorest 30 per cent of the population to appear in the studio discussion of poverty is a sign of this. The discussion among the *Newsnight* team is in some respects quite disturbing. The comment, 'They're so deprived they can't string two sentences together!' speaks volumes about how rarely working-class voices are heard on 'serious' current affairs programmes such as *Newsnight*. The process of 'casting' seems to conform to very unadventurous ideas of what a discussion about poverty might involve. There is a strong sense of tokenism in the inclusion of one 'poor person' amidst the politicians and the representative of the Church poverty pressure group. The idea that those involved in advocating for the poor are too suspicious of the media to appear on *Newsnight* seems dubious: can it really be so hard to find sources on such a key issue? Yet much of the humour in the *Newsnight* team's repartee seems to be directed back at themselves, for being so cut off. Star presenter Jeremy Paxman's comments draw attention to this (see Figure 2.9). He and Tania the producer almost seem to be saying, 'isn't this pathetic, how hard we find it to bring a working-class person into the studio?' The laughter at the 'crudity' of using film of 'kids with rickets' may be about the difficulty of representing poverty in a way that does not echo the conventions of the 'old' Reithian BBC. Humour, then, seems to be a way of dealing with the contradictions between serving the public and addressing only a small part of that public.

Figure 2.9 *Jeremy Paxman, presenter of* Newsnight *and probably the UK's best-known serious journalist*

Born does not comment on this extract, other than to set it against a quotation from one of the BBC's audit documents, its 'Statement of promises to listeners and viewers'. This quotation read: 'The BBC met its specific promise to: represent all groups in society accurately and avoid reinforcing prejudice in our programmes' (Born, 2002, p.67). Born is clearly suggesting that, while the language of audit sees such issues as targets to be met, creative staff struggle with real dilemmas and difficulties involved in making public service broadcasting. The diary extract also reveals what Born describes as the 'ambivalence' of the neo-Reithian counter-discourse. She seems to intend this term in something like its use in psychoanalysis: 'the simultaneous existence of contradictory tendencies, attitudes or feelings in the relationship to a single object – especially the coexistence of love and hate' (Laplanche and Pontalis, 1988, p.26). BBC staff were, to put it another way, torn over Reithianism.

This emphasis on the inner dynamics of institutions suggests how far we have moved methodologically from Herman and Chomsky's propaganda model, and from Hall et al.'s *Policing the Crisis*, where the study of what media producers say and do is irrelevant. Born's ethnographic approach homes right in on the views of media producers. The emphasis on reflexivity and ambivalence provides important clues about Born's views of the autonomy and independence of media producers. Even in the face of the most sustained attempts to introduce the profit imperative into every aspect of BBC work, and to make programme makers adhere to standards of accountability brought in from the world of commerce, workers at the BBC maintain a critical, anxious commitment to independence. This does not mean full autonomy from the profit imperative and from the state. Nor does it mean that such reflexivity always results in creative programme making or in texts that cast light on important facets of contemporary societies (such as poverty). But Born's analysis suggests the continuing existence of spaces where relative independence can exist.

What is Born's conception of the relationships between media production, media texts and power? This is not altogether clear in the piece under consideration (which focuses on particular issues of production), but there is a strong sense that media producers need to be understood as active *agents* in forging a variety of possible relationships, and that citizens need to be engaged in debates about the conditions for creativity in media production organisations, and about what constitutes aesthetic and ethical vitality in modern societies.

7 Conclusion

Let me now summarise the main issues covered in this chapter (see Table 2.1). I have compared five different approaches to the study of media organisations, in terms of their views of the relationship between media production, texts and power. I have traced the different perspectives each study took of the independence or autonomy of media producers from external control by powerful interests in society. Each looks at media organisations in different degrees of detail, and I have also briefly compared the methods underlying the different studies – how they gathered and interpreted their evidence, and which evidence they chose to highlight.

Table 2.1 Summary of approaches in Chapter 2

Approach	Production as propaganda	Producers as secondary definers	Production as contested field	Production as cultural process	Producers as reflexive
Authors	Herman and Chomsky	Hall et al.	Schlesinger and Tumber	Negus	Born
Range of examples covered	Foreign news reporting (press and TV)	News reporting on crime (in terms of youth and 'race')	Crime reporting	Rap (and other popular music genres)	Television production
Conceptions of 'autonomy'	Autonomy mostly an illusion; only possible in 'alternative' institutions	Producers not autonomous, 'cued in' to primary definitions by powerful sources	Relatively autonomous, can choose among competing sources, but subject to increasingly professional PR methods	Very much dependent on wider social (cultural?) processes	Stresses relative autonomy in form of reflexivity of producers, and their 'ambivalence'
Methods	Content analysis, plus secondary sources on media production	Content analysis, media production processes assumed; main focus very wide	Interviews with media workers, sources and some content analysis; production and texts rarely combined	Interviews with media workers, very little concern with texts	Ethnography, including interviews; interest in 'ethical and aesthetic vitality' of texts

Think back over the studies examined in this chapter, with the help of Table 2.1. To what extent do these studies support the view that media operate autonomously of powerful interests in society? ■ ■ ■

The research we have looked at provides some evidence that media producers do not operate as independently of the interests of powerful groups as many of them claim. Some of this evidence relies on textual analysis (such as Herman and Chomsky's analyses of news stories) and a detailed examination of strategies of textual analysis falls outside the remit of this book (see **Gillespie and Toynbee, 2006**). But studies of media production can provide analyses of the processes by which such texts end up taking the form that they do. Herman and Chomsky took the view that news coverage of war and foreign conflict overwhelmingly favoured the military and political interests of the USA and its allies. They suggested a number of factors ('filters') which, in their view, helped to ensure that other perspectives were not properly reported. The studies of crime by Hall et al. and by Schlesinger and Tumber showed that crime reporting tends to be heavily affected by the interests of the police and the criminal justice system. Negus showed that even in the case of rap, a successful African-American musical genre, media organisations (in the form of the big record companies) tended to reinforce existing patterns of ethnic inequality in US society as a whole, by marginalising rap as compared with rock. Lastly, Born portrayed even the most 'investigative' of news and current affairs television programmes struggling to find a working-class person to speak about the experience of poverty.

However, there were important differences between the studies we have looked at, especially over how they conceived of the relationship between social power and media production. Some stressed autonomy more than others. Herman and Chomsky saw this autonomy as extremely limited, because of the various economic and ideological filters they identified. Schlesinger and Tumber, like Hall et al., saw the sources used by crime journalists as ways in which the news could be shaped in accordance with dominant interests, but emphasised contestation among sources, and the increasingly skilful use of news management by alternative sources. Negus was pessimistic about the status of black music in predominantly white record companies, suggesting that autonomy was highly limited. Born, however, provides some evidence that autonomy is still possible in public service organisations, even those as relentlessly monitored and audited by senior managers as was the BBC in the 1990s.

There is a considerable range of views, then, and they should not be summed up glibly. None of the studies aspires to provide a portrait of the media as a whole (though Herman and Chomsky sometimes lean in that direction); each piece of research focuses on a particular aspect of media production. Together, these pieces of research allow us to build up an understanding of relations between social power and the media as complex and multifaceted. But this does not mean that these relations are so complex and multifaceted that it is impossible to speak of the media's role in reproducing inequalities and power differences in modern societies. On the contrary, all the writers here are critical of the media. Nevertheless, we should be wary of simple generalisations about media and power, on the part of either those who would say that the media are always mere servants of big business or the state, or of those who would say that producers operate independently of powerful interests. To take the first view would carry the disempowering implication that media reform was impossible, and to take the second view would be naively complacent. Both views fly in the face of much of the research discussed above.

Further reading

Boyd-Barrett, O. and Newbold, C. (eds) (1995) *Approaches to Media: A Reader*, London, Arnold. This general collection of work on the media contains a very good section of classic articles on media occupations and professions, much of which is relevant to the issues covered by this chapter.

Cottle, S. (ed.) (2003) *Media Organization and Production*, London, Sage. Curran, J. (ed.) (2000) *Media Organisations in Society*, London, Arnold. Two collections of essays on a wide range of media organisations, in a variety of international settings. Both are introduced by overviews of the field of study.

Deacon, D. and Golding, P. (1994) *Taxation and Representation: The Media, Political Communication and the Poll Tax*, London, John Libbey & Company. Like Schlesinger and Tumber, Deacon and Golding qualify the model of 'primary definition'. They show how the Conservative government, a highly accredited primary source, became discredited, partly as a result of dissensus among elite groups.

Frith, S. (1983) *Sound Effects: Youth, Leisure and the Politics of Rock 'n' Roll*, London, Constable. This older study remains a brilliant analysis of power, production and meaning, drawing on cultural studies and political economy thinking.

References

Born, G. (2002) 'Reflexivity and ambivalence: culture, creativity and government in the BBC', *Cultural Values*, vol.6, no.1/2, pp.65–90.

Bourdieu, P. (1996) *The Rules of Art*, Cambridge, Polity.

Braham, P. and Janes, L. (eds) (2002) *Social Differences and Divisions*, Oxford, Blackwell/The Open University.

Chomsky, N. (1989) *Necessary Illusions: Thought Control in Democratic Societies*, Toronto, CBC.

Corner, J. (2003) 'The model in question', *European Journal of Communication*, vol.18, no.3, pp.367–75.

Curran, J. and Seaton, J. (2003) *Power without Responsibility: The Press, Broadcasting and New Media in Britain* (6th edn), London, Routledge.

Du Gay, P. (ed.) (1997) *Production of Culture/Cultures of Production*, London, Sage/The Open University.

Ericson, R., Baranek, P. and Chan, J. (1989) *Negotiating Control*, Milton Keynes, Open University Press.

Frith, S. (1983) *Sound Effects: Youth, Leisure and the Politics of Rock 'n' Roll*, London, Constable.

Galtung, J. and Ruge, M.H. (1965) 'The structure of foreign news: the presentation of the Congo, Cuba and Cyprus crises in four foreign newspapers', *Journal of International Peace Research*, vol.1, pp.64–90.

Giddens, A. (1990) *The Consequences of Modernity*, Cambridge, Polity.

Gillespie, M. (2005) 'Television, drama and audience ethnography' in Gillespie, M. (ed.) *Media Audiences*, Maidenhead, Open University Press/The Open University (Book 2 in this series).

Gillespie, M. and Toynbee, J. (eds) (2006) *Analysing Media Texts*, Maidenhead, Open University Press/The Open University (Book 4 in this series).

Golding, P. and Murdock, G. (2000) 'Culture, communications and political economy' in Curran, J. and Gurevitch, M. (eds) *Mass Media and Society* (3rd edn), London, Arnold.

Hall, S., Critcher, C., Jefferson, T., Clarke, J. and Roberts, B. (1978) *Policing the Crisis: Mugging, the State, and Law and Order*, London and Basingstoke, Macmillan.

Hallin, D. (1986) *The 'Uncensored War': The Media and Vietnam*, Berkeley, CA, University of California Press.

Herman, E. (2000) 'The propaganda model: a retrospective', *Journalism Studies,* vol.1, no.1, pp.101–12.

Herman, E. and Chomsky, N. (1988) *Manufacturing Consent: The Political Economy of the Mass Media*, New York, Pantheon.

Hesmondhalgh, D. (2006) 'Discourse analysis and content analysis' in Gillespie, M. and Toynbee, J. (eds) *Analysing Media Texts*, Maidenhead, Open University Press/The Open University (Book 4 in this series).

Klaehn, J. (2002) 'A critical review and assessment of Herman and Chomsky's "propaganda model"', *European Journal of Communication,* vol.17, no.2, pp.147–82.

Laplanche, J. and Pontalis, J.B. (1988) *The Language of Psychoanalysis*, London, Karnac.

Negus, K. (1998) 'Cultural production and the corporation: musical genres and the strategic management of creativity in the US recording industry', *Media, Culture and Society,* vol.20, pp.359–79.

Negus, K. (1999) *Music Genres and Corporate Cultures*, London, Routledge.

Savage, M. (2002) 'Social exclusion and class analysis' in Braham, P. and Janes, L. (eds) *Social Differences and Divisions*, Oxford, Blackwell/The Open University.

Schlesinger, P. (1987) *Putting 'Reality' Together*, London, Routledge.

Schlesinger, P. (1990) 'Rethinking the sociology of journalism: source strategies and the limits of media-centrism' in Ferguson, M. (ed.) *Public Communication: The New Imperatives*, London, Sage.

Schlesinger, P. and Tumber, H. (1994) *Reporting Crime: The Media Politics of Criminal Justice*, Oxford, Clarendon.

Wacquant, L. (2002) 'From slavery to mass incarceration: rethinking the "race question" in the US', *New Left Review,* vol.13 (2nd series), pp.41–60.

Weaver, D. and Wilhoit, G. (1991) *The American Journalist* (2nd edn), Bloomington, IN, University of Indiana Press.

White, D.M. (1950) 'The gatekeeper: a case study in the selection of news', *Journalism Quarterly,* vol.27, pp.383–90.

The media's view of the audience

Jason Toynbee

Contents

1   Introduction

There is a paradox about the development of the modern media. On the one hand, because they are located at the hub of large distribution networks, media organisations are in an ideal position to know the audience and collate information about it. In effect, newspaper publishers, television stations and record companies have a bird's-eye view of their readers, viewers or listeners. On the other hand, the very opposite tendency seems to be at work. By definition, the development of the mass media has involved putting distance between producers and audiences over both time and space. What is more, media audiences are large and their members are often shut away behind the closed doors of the household. As a result, producers of media messages tend to be unsure about how they are being received, or even whether anyone is paying attention at all.

Over the course of this chapter I will examine the nature of this paradox and the ways in which the media industries have tried to deal with it by using techniques of audience research and measurement. As is always the case in media studies there is a debate here. In this case it is a particularly intense debate because the problems of how far the media can know the audience, of gathering information and gauging the effects of using it, bear on a central question in media studies. To what extent can the media industries be said to have power over the audience? In particular, does the research that they commission increase that power or, on the contrary, encourage greater responsiveness to the wishes and interests of media users?

The shape of the chapter is formed by the lines of this debate, with Sections 2 to 4 each examining a key position in it. Then, in Section 5, I turn to the question of stability and change, and consider whether the role of research has shifted in recent years, becoming more significant and contributing to the conglomeration of media companies as well as the fragmentation of traditional audiences.

We can start by looking in outline at the key positions. The first (outlined in Section 2) is an argument put forward chiefly by the media industries, advertising agencies and market researchers themselves, which makes the case for the *effectiveness* of audience research (Miller, 1994). The media, it is suggested, have developed reliable methods for finding out how many people are attending to which texts. Moreover, these methods have been refined to keep pace with shifting patterns in media use and new technologies in the home – the internet and cable television, for example. As a result, media organisations are able to continuously update their knowledge of the audience and, using this information, can satisfy changing demand for genres, celebrities, forms of advertising, and so on. We might describe this as a market liberal position (see Chapter 1).

It emphasises the facility of the media to provide different things for different people, as well as the functionality of a market in which plenty of information enables choices by consumers and matching responses from producers.

This position is then challenged by a second approach (outlined in Section 3), which takes almost the opposite line. Writers from the critical political economy school suggest that audience research by the media is really a form of *exploitation* (for more about political economy, once again see Chapter 1; see also **Hesmondhalgh, 2005**). In its strongest form – for instance, the work of Dallas Smythe (1995/1981) – the argument goes that the audience effectively works for the media, transforming itself into a commodity that is then sold to advertisers. What the advertisers are buying is actually the attention of potential consumers for their products. In this context audience research serves to quantify and package audiences, making them saleable.

Third, and in contrast to both the above approaches, some scholars have proposed that audience research undertaken by the media suffers from chronic *failure* (this is outlined in Section 4). Of course, media organisations always assert that their research produces true knowledge. But the fact is, according to these sceptics, it does not. The reason is that real audiences interpret messages in their own way, sometimes paying attention, and sometimes ignoring the texts they are supposed to be attending to. In suggesting this Ien Ang builds on a very different tradition of audience research: the ethnographic approach in media studies, to which she herself has contributed (Ang, 1991; see also **Gillespie, 2005**). Here qualitative research, involving in-depth interviews and observation, has shown that people interact with television in quite complex and multifarious ways. As Ang argues in her case study of television, the result is that the forms of measurement adopted by audience researchers working for the media invariably produce a false picture.

Clearly the three positions that I have just outlined diverge strongly from each other. Yet there is something they have in common. All three recognise that *uncertainty* lies at the heart of the mass communications process (cf. **Hesmondhalgh, 2005**). The differences are really to do with judgements about how far media organisations overcome uncertainty and what they do with knowledge of the audience – to the extent that they achieve it. So, why is uncertainty such an important issue for the media?

One factor has come up already: the distance between producers and audiences across time and space. If you think about an example of face-to-face communication, say a market trader calling out to a crowd in front of her stall, this is not a problem of course. The trader can watch people's bodies, look for a reaction and then make adjustments to her turn of phrase and tone of voice so as to maximise her appeal. In the case of the media, though, such instant knowledge of the audience is just not possible because of the enormous distance between senders and receivers of messages. More than this, as sociologists have been pointing out since the 1930s, the media audience is atomised, consisting of anonymous individuals from different social backgrounds who are physically removed from one another (Blumer, 1966) (see Figure 3.1). More recently, John Thompson has drawn on this 'mass' audience approach, in order to develop a more sophisticated view of the relationship between media and audience, which he calls 'mediated quasi-interaction'. It is characterised by four main features: one-way communication, the spatial segregation of production from reception, the repeatability of messages and an 'orientation towards an indefinite range of potential recipients' (Thompson, 1995, p.85). Each of these factors on its own would make it difficult to know for sure who the audience is, what it is attending to and how it is reacting. Together they provide a serious challenge for media organisations.

Figure 3.1 *The new atomised mass media audience: a radio listener in the early 1920s*

As well as problems of distance and mediation, uncertainty about audiences also derives from the difficulty of predicting demand for media products. Creative artefacts are 'experience goods', in other words they need to be read, watched or listened to before the user can tell whether she or he likes them. This has to do with the complexity of even the most standardised media output – the fact there are so many dimensions to it. In the case of a new pop single, for example, perception of the voice quality of the singer is clearly important. But so is melody and the way the song builds dynamically over its length, not to mention that line in the chorus that is supposed to stick in your head. I could go on adding more dimensions indefinitely, each one of which might, but equally might not, enter into the equation of value made by audience members. The point is that the 'infinite variety' at stake here makes it very difficult for media organisations to predict in advance of publication those products audiences will like (Caves, 2001, p.6).

Activity 3.1

Imagine you are starting up a small publishing firm or a record label covering a specialist area: sports books perhaps, or indie rock. Bear in mind those factors of distance, mediation and uncertainty that I have just been discussing. Then think about the following questions and note down your responses to them.

- ■ What do you need to know about your potential audience?
- ■ What techniques could you use to find out about it?
- ■ To what use will you put the information that you have gathered? ■ ■ ■

Activity 3.1 should be helpful when it comes to examining the case studies in media audience research later in the chapter. The questions you have been addressing are key questions for all media organisations. But perhaps they are less straightforward than they appear at first sight. For one thing, it is likely that, by thinking about a 'potential audience' you have already started actively to imagine one, to assume a particular character and constitution for it. Equally, the choice of research techniques will contribute to the way in which your audience is defined. This is a problem we will encounter in several places: that doing research involves not just showing phenomena or collecting information, but also constructing knowledge. The third question in Activity 3.1 points up this problem and brings us to the final issue we need to consider in this Introduction, namely the purposes of media audience research and the interests that it serves.

Broadly speaking, public service media – notably public service broadcasting (PSB) organisations such as the BBC – have a different interest in audience research from commercial media. In principle, at least, PSB addresses its audience as citizens rather than consumers. It follows that an important reason for doing research here is to show the reach and effectiveness of those programmes that in some sense prioritise public service and civic values. This will be broadcasting that informs, educates and entertains and that, to think about it in a slightly different way, promotes democratic and liberal values. Ultimately then, PSB audience research is intended to show the vigour of PSB to the citizens and governments who pay for it and ensure its existence. In recent times the shape and nature of PSB has been called into question by the rise of commercial multi-channel broadcasting that threatens to swamp it, and by differences of opinion about whether PSB is still needed. This has made research by public service media organisations even more urgent. They need to demonstrate the special value of PSB to citizens, yet also its continued ability to reach a mass audience whose members pay for public service programmes through licence fees or taxes.

In commercially funded media we can identify two approaches to audience research. Where the main income is derived from sales or subscription (as with books, CDs, films and cable television) the aim is to gain knowledge of audience preferences simply in order to maximise the number of people who buy. With advertising-funded media, such as broadcast commercial television or the press, as already suggested, the goal is rather different, namely to sell the audience to advertisers. In this case research should show to what extent the audience matches the market for the product that the advertiser is promoting, in terms of size and composition. In both cases, however, the essentially commercial reasons for trying to find out about the audience are very different from the civic or democracy-supporting values that inform audience research in PSB.

I have now sketched out a framework for the chapter and examined some of the basic conditions that shape audience research in modern media systems. The next step is to examine in more detail the key positions in the debate about knowing the audience. We can begin with the view from the media.

2   The media's view of audience research

At the most general level the argument for audience research is that media organisations need to find out what the audience likes so that they can shape output accordingly. Quite simply, producing audio-visual and print material that no one wants is a waste of resources. This essentially economic argument for audience research has a particular force in the case of the media because ('sunk') production costs are very high compared with the ('marginal') costs of reproduction: in other words, distribution or transmission. So, for example, if a magazine fails then the huge amounts of money invested in setting it up are lost. The same goes for a film or television show, indeed all media products. In this context audience research reduces the risk of failure, so making for efficiency and the best use of scarce resources. What is more, in a market environment, research encourages competition between different media producers, each of whom will use information about audience preferences to maximise the desirability of what they offer.

2.1 Pretesting the product

The process of obtaining market information begins with 'pretesting', a form of audience research carried out before a product is properly released and large-scale resources have been committed to developing it. It is intended precisely to reduce that demand uncertainty that we examined earlier.

Reading 3.1 Activity

Now read the following extract from Philip Napoli's (2003) book, *Audience Economics* (Reading 3.1). In this extract he describes various kinds of pretesting of media products used in the USA. Please read the extract now and consider these questions:

- What is meant by 'representativeness', and why is it an issue?
- How might the results of piloting be used by media producers?
- Is the pretest a suitable form of market research for all kinds of media?
- How successful do you think pretesting of media products is likely to be in relation to the goal of satisfying consumer preferences?

Reading 3.1

Philip Napoli, 'Pretesting media products'

One prominent way that participants in the audience market attempt to cope with uncertainty is by pretesting content on 'sample' audiences and then using the feedback to generate predictions of the media product's performance. For instance, the magazine industry conducts audience simulations for yet-to-be-published magazines (Miller, 1994). These simulations involve developing circulation numbers by using such data as the new magazine's publishing philosophy, target audience, and the circulation numbers for similar magazines in the marketplace.

Television programmers have for years conducted 'pilot testing' for their new programs. In many instances the data derived from these tests are a central factor in determining whether a program makes it on the air [...]. Pilot tests involve showing the first episode of a new program (the pilot) to audiences and then recording their reactions, typically through theater testing or in-home cable testing. Theater testing involves recruiting a reasonably representative sample audience to attend a theater screening of a program. After the screening the programmer uses questionnaires and focus groups to record the audience's reaction to the program. Theater testing also uses what is known as 'dial testing'. In dial tests audience members use a device that allows them to register their level of satisfaction with the program while they are viewing it. Viewers turn the dial in one direction if they are enjoying what they are seeing and the opposite direction if they are dissatisfied. These individual responses are then aggregated to produce what looks like a minute-by-minute electrocardiogram of the program. Newer versions of the dial-test technology even include a 'tune-out' button, which audience members can press to register the specific point at which they no longer wish to view the program (Greene, 2000). These data can be used not only to decide whether to air a program but also to edit out or reshoot poorly received scenes or to drop or recast entire characters, if their appearance on screen coincides with low levels of satisfaction among the audience members (Gitlin, 1994/1983; Greene, 2000). [...]

Despite its prominence as an analytical tool for programmers, theater testing is not without its flaws. First, the degree to which a small theater audience recruited off the street accurately represents the viewing audience as a whole has major limitations (Gitlin, 1994/1983). Interestingly, researchers have found that Las Vegas, with its mix of families, young singles, retirees, and conventioneers from all over the country, provides them with the best opportunity for constructing a geographically and demographically representative test audience [...]. Nonetheless, representativeness remains a major limitation. In addition, many critics have noted that theater tests do not reflect the typical media consumption environment. That is, watching a program in a theater with a group of strangers is fundamentally different from watching a program in the comfort of one's own home, with friends or family. Consequently, whether theater test audiences are watching and responding to programs in a frame of mind that accurately reflects how they watch – and respond to – television programs at home is questionable.

In-home cable testing involves recruiting a sample of viewers and instructing them to watch a particular cable channel at a particular time. In conjunction with the local cable system, the programmer then transmits the test program at the designated time. After the broadcast, testers interview the participants by telephone to get their reactions to the program (Stipp and Schiavone, 1990).

Cable testing addresses some weaknesses of the theater testing approach but also has unique shortcomings. Unlike theater tests, cable testing does allow viewers to watch and evaluate a program within the comfort of their own home. In addition, cable testing permits construction of a much larger viewing audience than is possible using theater testing. However, representativeness is once again an issue, given that roughly 30 percent of the television audience does not subscribe to cable. These viewers are thus unreachable via the cable testing method. In addition, not all cable systems are willing to participate, which introduces the possibility of further distortions in the geographic and demographic mix of participants. [...]

Radio uses similar pretesting techniques. Researchers use a variety of methods to pretest the appeal of individual songs. One approach, called 'call out' studies, involves playing small segments of songs (called 'hooks') over the telephone to a random sample of respondents and collecting their feedback ([...] MacFarland, 1997). 'Call-in' studies involve contacting participants by mail, then having them phone in to a designated number to listen to a series of hooks and provide feedback by either mail or telephone. The criticism of these approaches is that the telephone represents a much lower level of sound quality than radio ([...] MacFarland, 1997). Radio researchers overcome the issue of sound quality by using auditorium studies, in which participants are recruited to a theater or auditorium to listen to a series of songs or hooks. However, the trade-off for providing better sound quality is that auditorium studies generally are too time consuming and too expensive to gain feedback from as many participants as is possible with call-in or call-out studies. Radio researchers also test the appeal of individual radio formats when a new station is entering the market or when an existing station is considering a change in format. Format research involves obtaining feedback from audience members (using both survey and focus group methods) about whether they are likely to listen to each of any number of format options (Hanson, 1991).

References

Gitlin, T. (1994/1983) *Inside Prime Time* (2nd edn), London, Routledge.

Greene, K. (2000) 'TV's test pilots', *Broadcasting & Cable*, vol.130, no.3, p.52.

Hanson, K. (1991) 'Format research' in Hartshorn, G. (ed.) *Audience Research Sourcebook*, Washington, DC, National Association of Broadcasters.

MacFarland, D. (1997) *Future Radio Programming Strategies: Cultivating Listenership in the Digital Age* (2nd edn), Mahwah, NJ, Lawrence Erlbaum.

Miller, P. (1994) 'Made-to-order and standardized audiences: forms of reality in audience measurement' in Ettema, J. and Whitney, D. (eds) *Audience Making: How the Media Create the Audience*, Thousand Oaks, CA, Sage.

Stipp, H. and Schiavone, N. (1990) 'Research at a commercial television network: NBC 1990', *Marketing Research*, vol.2, no.3, pp.3–10.

Reading source

Napoli, 2003, pp.40–3 ■ ■ ■

The pretest is a key part of audience research in several sectors of the media, but as you were working through the questions of Reading Activity 3.1 it may already have occurred to you that there are limits to the applicability of the pretest. In some markets rates of innovation are high – styles change quickly; and in some cases the number of media products (the catalogue) is particularly large. Both conditions apply in the recording industry and book publishing, and this accounts for the fact that there is no piloting here. It is simply impossible to pretest 'one-off' products – such as singles, albums or books – which are released in their hundreds each month. Instead, there is a combination of reliance on the 'gut feeling' of industry personnel about new trends, with a careful monitoring of responses to new releases as they are issued (for the record industry see Negus, 1999).

If pretesting only occurs in certain sectors, all media undertake research on audiences of the actual, rather than potential, kind. Media organisations that sell products directly to the public – once again, print publishing and the recording industry – have a certain advantage here. With the increasing use of computerised, electronic point of sale (EPOS) systems in shops they can accurately record how many copies of books, records or periodicals are bought. In the case of cable television or satellite pay-TV the equivalent information is the number of subscribers as recorded by the electronic billing system. Sales or subscription statistics are certainly useful to the media. Yet in an important sense they do not measure the audience. This is because a single copy or subscription service can be watched by many. Magazines, for example, are passed around and read much more widely than sales figures would suggest. And that matters because the bulk of magazine revenue comes from advertising. Advertisers want to know *which* people read what and *how often*, rather than simple sales figures. As a result, media that make direct sales to the public generally commission more comprehensive audience research to supplement their sales statistics. For broadcast radio, television and websites, of course, there are no sales figures to begin with, so specially designed research is the only way of finding out about the audience.

2.2 Ratings and responsiveness

What is involved in doing media audience research? It might be best to address this question through a case study. US broadcast television, with its nationwide networks, many local stations and huge audience targeted by the biggest advertising industry in the world, has the most highly developed audience research of any commercial media system. Most importantly, many features of US television research are found in other sectors and other places. So, let us take it as our example.

The paramount issue confronting television companies is the need for accuracy, or rather, the need to *show* that the results of research are an accurate measure of the actual audience. In particular, broadcasters have to persuade sceptical advertisers that the audience is as big as they claim it is. To this end an independent research organisation is hired in order to minimise the charge of bias. In the USA it is Nielsen Media Research. The commissioning of third-party research and the co-operation that is required in order for this to be agreed between parties with conflicting interests (the competing television networks, but also advertisers) enables a strong claim to objectivity. Here is a case where the commercial rationale for research tends to maximise authenticity because 'media buyers' – the advertisers – demand that audience research is non-partisan (Miller, 1994).

The first step in conducting research is to choose a sample. In Reading Activity 3.1 we looked at representativeness in the context of pretesting. The issue was how media firms might ensure that a tiny pilot audience represented the potential market for a media product. In actual audience research this problem of sampling becomes critical. For reasons of cost it is only possible for a small cross-section of the audience to be targeted. But how should it be selected? Several factors are important here. First is size. The sample has to be big enough so that it will adequately represent the actual audience. For its national network research, Nielsen seeks responses from around 5,000 of the 100 million households with television in the USA. In statistical terms this is sufficiently large, but the problem then becomes one of ensuring randomness so that no particular audience segment (by gender, ethnicity, age, income, etc.) will be over-represented or under-represented. Sampling is done in two stages. First, 6,000 small geographical units are randomly selected and then, within these, there is a further random selection of households. Nielsen is very keen to point to the inclusiveness that results from using techniques like these. In particular, the company argues, minority ethnic groups are not left out, but rather are recognised to the extent that separate viewing figures are published for African-American and Hispanic audiences (Nielsen Media Research, 2004).

Once the sample has been selected, research can begin. Immediately, though, an even bigger question crops up, namely *how* to gather information about what is being watched. In fact two main methods have emerged historically. The first is the audience diary. This paper booklet is filled in by a named member of the household who records what is being watched over a seven-day period. Now used mainly for research into local television as well as for radio audiences, diaries are a cheap form of research and so can be used on a broad basis in markets in which the relatively low value of the audience to advertisers precludes more expensive, automated techniques. However, diaries suffer from several problems. Perhaps the main one is that respondents tend not to note down their entries until the last minute before the diaries have to be sent off. This means that entries may be made on the basis of a hazy memory of viewing up to a week in the past. What is more, and this is particularly true if the respondent does much channel hopping, filling in a diary is a tedious and complicated business, whether done 'on the spot' or at a later time. Not surprisingly, this results in under-recording. Finally, diaries privilege the well known programmes on the major networks, which tend to be more easily remembered (Napoli, 2003, pp.88–9).

The other main research technique, the use of a meter connected to the television set, eliminates many of these problems (see Figure 3.2). Since 1987 Nielsen have used the 'people meter' for national, network audience research. This device not only continuously records which channel is selected while the television is switched on, but also enables a degree of individuation among household members. Respondents are asked to use their own dedicated handset to indicate when they begin and finish watching television. The meter also shows the demographic characteristics of each person, and in this way a more nuanced, yet reliable, method of measuring the audience is achieved.

Significantly, the introduction of the people meter revealed that cable television was much more popular than had previously been assumed. As a result, advertising in the medium increased, so driving up revenue and, in turn, the launch of more cable channels. The people meter also showed that men, children and teenagers watched a greater amount of television than had been thought before. Finally, the more detailed demographic information being collected enabled the development of carefully targeted programmes that reflected the interests of particular social groups (Napoli, 2003, pp.91–2). The story of the people meter seems, then, to bear out the market liberal

Figure 3.2 *Television with 'people meter' attached (see top right)*

justification for audience research. Improvements in research techniques lead to improvements in the quality of television and greater satisfaction of the audience, as well as the recognition of previously 'invisible' groups.

It should be clear by now that television audience research in the USA (as elsewhere) is pre-eminently quantitative. It generates numbers of *people* watching *programmes* or *stations* at particular *times*. But in what ways are these numbers expressed? The term used in the industry to describe different kinds of audience measure is 'metric'. Here are some of the key metrics.

- HUT (households using television): percentage of the television households in a given market (national, local, cable, etc.) with a television switched on.
- Share: percentage of the HUT tuned to a particular station.
- Rating: percentage of the television households in a given market (that is, all households with a television, rather than households with a television switched on as in the case of the share) tuned to a particular station.
- GRPs (gross rating points): sum of ratings in a time slot (for example, Mondays, 8 p.m. to 9 p.m.) or an advertisement spot (for example, McDonalds advertisements) over a certain period (for example, a month).

- Reach: percentage of television households that have tuned into a channel, programme or advertisement at least once over a certain period.
- Frequency: average number of times a household tuned into a channel, programme or advertisement over a certain period; calculated by dividing GRPs by reach figure.

Perhaps the most important implication of the *variety* of metrics described above, is that the US television industry is keen to measure its audience comprehensively, and to do this in ways of which advertisers can make maximum use. In Activity 3.2, we will examine some audience figures and carry out a few elementary calculations in order to become more familiar with their statistical meaning and industrial application.

Activity 3.2

Tables 3.1 and 3.2 below show audience figures for the top ten programmes on US national, network television in two successive weeks. Study these tables and then answer the questions that follow.

Table 3.1 19–24 January, 2004 (Week 1)

Rank	Programme name	Network	Time/Day	Rating	Share	Households*
1	Golden Globe Awards	NBC	8:00 p.m. Sun	16.9	25.0	18,347.000
2	American Idol – Tuesday	FOX	8:00 p.m. Tue	16.2	24.0	17,550.000
3	American Idol – Wednesday	FOX	8:00 p.m. Wed	16.2	25.0	17,561.000
4	American Idol – PRM Spec(s)	FOX	8:00 p.m. Mon	15.9	23.0	17,214.000
5	Friends	NBC	8:00 p.m. Thu	13.4	21.0	14,488.000
6	CSI	CBS	9:01 p.m. Thu	13.2	20.0	14,285.000
7	Friends	NBC	8:32 p.m. Thu	13.1	20.0	14,218.000
8	Big Fat Obnoxious Fiancé	FOX	9:08 p.m. Mon	11.6	17.0	12,525.000
9	CSI: Miami	CBS	10:00 p.m. Mon	10.6	17.0	11,542.000
10	Will & Grace	NBC	9:02 p.m. Thu	10.4	16.0	11,305.000

NB: * That is, number of households watching the programme.

Source: http://tv.yahoo.com/nielsen/ (accessed 2 February 2004)

Table 3.2 26 January to 1 February, 2004 (Week 2)

Rank	Programme name	Network	Time/Day	Rating	Share	Households*
1	Super Bowl XXXVIII	CBS	6:27 p.m. Sun	41.4	63.0	44,908,000
2	Super Bowl Post Game	CBS	10:33 p.m. Sun	28.8	46.0	31,243,000
3	Survivor: All-Stars	CBS	10:52 p.m. Sun	17.9	32.0	19,415,000
4	American Idol – Tues	FOX	8:00 p.m. Tue	16.7	24.0	18,055,000
5	American Idol – Weds	FOX	8:00 p.m. Wed	15.7	24.0	17,058,000
6	Friends	NBC	8:00 p.m. Thu	13.3	21.0	14,442,000
7	CSI	CBS	9:01 p.m. Thu	13.0	19.0	14,085,000
8	Apprentice	NBC	9:00 p.m. Thu	11.9	18.0	12,944,000
9	Without A Trace	CBS	10:00 p.m. Thu	11.5	19.0	12,492,000
10	Will & Grace	NBC	8:32 p.m. Thu	11.2	17.0	12,109,000

NB: * That is, number of households watching the programme.

Source: http://tv.yahoo.com/nielsen/ (accessed 2 February, 2004)

- Can you calculate the HUT level during the screening of *Without a Trace* in Week 2? (Hint: if you cannot deduce the formula for this calculation – and the author of this chapter couldn't on his own – go to the end of this chapter.)
- Can you explain how in Week 1 *Big Fat Obnoxious Fiancé* has the same share as, yet a rating one point higher than, *CSI Miami*?
- Assuming broadly similar ratings for the *Super Bowl* (the annual US football final) in previous years, what might be the economic implications of screening it for broadcasters and advertisers? ■ ■ ■

Activity 3.2 should have helped you to think about the way Nielsen ratings 'frame' the audience, and the kinds of use the statistics are put to. But notwithstanding its crucial role in television economics, this large-scale syndicated research (so called because it is paid for by a group of businesses) is not the only type encountered in the field. Individual stations or production houses also commission specially designed research for their own programmes. This is generally qualitative in its approach; in other words, it seeks to find out about the value judgements and subjective experience of audience members through relatively unstructured techniques such as in-depth interviews. For instance, one research company carries out tailored focus-group research for the television industry in which participants are asked not only about which programmes they like but also why they like them. In contrast to the random sampling of the Nielsen system, purposive sampling is used, with participants being selected on the grounds of their likely receptivity to specific programmes or advertisements (Audience Research and Development, 2004). In principle at least, this type of research enables the difficult questions of audience responsiveness and recall to be addressed. Discussion can tease out nuances, or even whole new aspects of audience engagement, which the crude metrics of ratings, shares, and so on can never get near to capturing.

This does not mean that such methods are in any straightforward sense *better* than the collation of syndicated ratings. Rather, Peter Miller argues, audience research should be conceived of as a dual system in which the strengths and weaknesses of each type 'play off against one another' (Miller, 1994, p.72). So, while data from custom research is relatively rich, and gets closer to representing the nature of an audience's engagement with television, it is not easily comparable with other research data. What is more, being specially commissioned it is open to the charge of partiality. In contrast, the information collected through syndicated research is comparatively poor. Yet it does at least facilitate comparison between different stations, programmes or periods. And the fact that it is syndicated enables a much stronger claim for objectivity to be made, as I discussed earlier.

We end this section about the media's view of knowing the audience, then, on an upbeat note. The case of the US television industry seems to suggest that research has become increasingly effective over the years, and that different types complement one another. The outcome is detailed knowledge of who watches which programmes, when and with what kind of attention. Such knowledge makes for efficiency, reduces uncertainty and enables television programming to be produced for audiences that are likely to be receptive to it. Meanwhile the costs of this expensive product are born by the advertisers.

3 Not so much research, more a form of exploitation: the critical political economy view

Academics working within the critical political economy view of the media (CPEM) look at things rather differently. Instead of seeing audience research as a means of making the media more responsive, they treat it as a form of manipulation. As in all kinds of rational argument this is partly a matter of marshalling evidence, of trying to demonstrate that it is the case. But CPEM also begins from a different premise, namely that the media industries need to be understood as institutions that have power over audiences. This power is not absolute, but it is nonetheless considerable. Where does it come from? Most of all, the argument goes, it derives from the fact that the handful of giant media corporations have an economic stranglehold. Their entrenched position of control over markets tends to lead to further encroachment as they squeeze out, or take over, other firms. The result is that competition is reduced, and alternative voices cannot be heard. There are structural reasons for this. Start-up costs are enormous in most areas of media production (most notably, film and television), and in all cases the setting up and running of distribution systems is prohibitively expensive for most new entrants. As a result only big capital can get a look in.

The nature of the audience and its relation to advertising has a crucial bearing here. For Nicholas Garnham (1990) the media industries not only produce commodities – programmes, books, CDs, films, and so on – they also have the key role of promoting them by means of advertising. As with other CPEM scholars, Garnham's use of the term commodity is derived from Marx for whom goods (or commodities) represent a key component of the capitalist system. It is their production and exchange that leads to the accumulation of capital. Through advertising, Garnham suggests, the media facilitate a wider process of 'commodification': more and more people buy more and more things. What we have here, then, is a strongly critical view of the role of the audience, one that sees it as the receiver of partisan messages promoting consumption.

Dallas Smythe (1995/1981) goes a step further. He argues that the media audience should not simply be seen as receptive to the message of the commodity (as Garnham suggests). Rather, its members have, in effect, to make themselves into consumers by actively choosing from an ever-expanding range of goods in the shops (and now, of course, on retail websites too). Attending to information about commodities, that is to say advertisements, is a vital part of this process. Crucially, it results in the audience itself becoming a commodity, to be sold on by the media to advertisers. Let us look at these ideas in more detail.

<h3>Reading 3.2 Activity</h3>

Now read the following extract, originally from Smythe's 1981 book, *Dependency Road* (Reading 3.2). As you read, think about these questions and make notes:

■ According to Smythe we *work* as members of the media audience to find out about the great range of consumer products that we encounter on a daily basis. This is a radical idea, but is it a helpful one? To what extent does it correspond to the way in which the media and advertising industries view the audience as being essentially economic in character? When thinking about the second part of the question it might be useful to have a look at some websites of advertising agencies or audience research firms.

■ If the audience is a commodity, as Smythe suggests, what exactly is being bought and sold, and what might be the role of audience research in relation to this commodity?

Reading 3.2

Dallas Smythe, 'On the audience commodity and its work'

What is the nature of the service performed for the advertiser by the members of the purchased audience? In economic terms, the audience commodity is a non-durable producer good which is bought and used in the marketing of the advertiser's product. The work which audience members perform for the advertiser to whom they have been sold is learning to buy goods and to spend their income accordingly. Sometimes, it is to buy any of the class of goods (e.g. an aircraft manufacturer is selling air transport in general, or the dairy industry, all brands of milk) but most often it is a particular 'brand' of consumer goods. In short, they work to create the demand for advertised goods which is the purpose of the monopoly-capitalist advertisers. Audience members may resist, but the advertiser's expectations are realized sufficiently that the results perpetuate the system of demand management.

People in audiences, we should remember, have had a rich history of education for their work as audience members. As children, teenagers, and adults they have observed old and new models of particular brands of products on the street, in homes of friends, at school, at the job front, etc. Much time will have been spent in discussing the 'good' and 'bad' features of brands of commodities in hundreds of contexts. A constant process of direct experience with commodities goes on and blends into all aspects of people's lives all the time. Advertisers get this huge volume of audience work (creation of consumer consciousness) as a bonus even before a specific media free-lunch-advertising programme appears on the tube face and initiates a new episode in audience work [...] .

The nature of audience work may best be approached through successive approximations. At the superficial level it looks like this: 'Customers do not buy things. They buy tools to solve problems', according to Professor T.N. Levitt (1976, p.73) of Harvard Business School. The nature of the work done by audience power thus seems to be to use the advertising-free-lunch combination of sensory stimuli to determine whether s/he (1) has the 'problem' the advertiser is posing (e.g. loneliness, sleeplessness, prospective economic insecurity for loved ones after the breadwinner's death, etc.), (2) is aware that there is a class of commodities which, if purchased and used will 'solve' that problem (e.g. shampoo, non-prescription sleeping drugs, life insurance) and that people like him/her use this class of commodity for this purpose, (3) ought to add brand X of that class of commodities to the mental or physical shopping list for the next trip to the store. This is the advertisers' rational basis. For audience members, however, their work is not so rational.

There is an *ever-increasing* number of decisions forced on audience members by new commodities and their related advertising. In addition to the many thousand of different items stocked by a typical supermarket at any one time, more than a thousand new consumer commodities appear each year. Literally millions of possible comparative choices face the audience member who goes shopping. [...]

Your work, as audience member, has to do with how your life's problems interact with the advertising-free-lunch experience. But how? How, in light of that experience do you decide whether you really have the 'problem' to which the advertiser has sought to sensitize you? And if the answer to this question be affirmative, how do you decide that the class of commodities which have been produced to cope with that problem will really serve their advertised purpose? And if the answer to that question be affirmative, how do you decide whether to buy brand A, B, or n? *The process contains a monstrous contradiction. It is totally rational from the advertisers' perspective and totally irrational from the audience members'.*

Faced with the necessity to make some decisions as to what classes and what brands of commodities to put on the shopping list (if only to preserve a shred of self-respect as one capable of making one's own decisions), it seems that Staffen B. Linder (1970, p.59) may be correct in saying that the most important way by which consumers can cope with commodities and advertising is to limit the time spent per purchase in thinking about what to buy:

> Reduced time for reflection previous to a decision would apparently entail a growing irrationality. However, since it is extremely rational to consider less and less per decision there exists a rationale of irrationality.

[...] How much time do most people spend as part of the audience product of the mass media – their time which is sold by the media to advertisers? David Blank, economist for the Columbia Broadcasting System, found in 1970 that the average person watched television for 3.3 hours per day (23 hours per week) on an annual basis, listened to radio for 2.5 hours per day (18 hours per week), and read newspapers and magazines for one hour per day (seven hours per week) (Blank, 1970). Recent years show similar magnitudes. If we look at the audience product in terms of families rather than individuals, we find that in 1973 advertisers in the United States purchased television audiences for an average of a little more than 43 hours per home per week (*Broadcasting Yearbook*, 1974, p.69). By industry usage, this lumps together specialized audience commodities sold independently as 'housewives', 'children' and 'families'. In the prime time evening hours (7:00 p.m. to 11:00 p.m.), the television audience commodity consisted of a daily average of 83.8 million people, with an average of two persons viewing per home. Women were a significantly higher proportion of this prime time audience than men (42 % as against 32 %; children were 16 %; teenagers 10 %).

Let us sum up these figures. Television, radio, and newspapers plus magazines take up 48 hours per week, for the average American! And they have only seven hours more free time than in 1850! Obviously some doubling up takes place. So let us estimate that half of the radio listening takes place while travelling to or from work; perhaps another quarter while doing the personal care chores at the beginning and end of the day. As for television, perhaps a fourth of it (on average) is glimpsed while preparing meals, eating, washing dishes, or doing other household tasks or repair/construction work. Estimate half of newspaper and magazine reading as taking place while travelling between home and job, while eating, etc. Our reduced exclusive audience time with the four commercial media is now down to 22 hours per week. Obviously more doubling takes place between audience time and other activities, and the reader is invited to make more precise estimates based on (perhaps) some empirical research. [...]

Perhaps the only conclusion to be drawn at this time on this point is that there is no free time devoid of audience activity which is not pre-empted by other activities which are market-related (including sleep which is necessary if you are to be fit to meet your market tests on the morrow). In *any* society, sleep and other non-work activities are necessary to restore and maintain life and labour power. Work itself is not intrinsically oppressive. It is the inclusion in so-called leisure time of commodity producing work under monopoly capitalism which creates the contradiction between oppressive and liberating activity in time for which people are not paid.

References

Blank, D.M. (1970) 'Pleasurable Pursuits – The Changing Structure of Leisure Time Spectator Activities', National Association of Business Economists, Annual Meeting September 1970 (unpublished paper).

Levitt, T.N. (1976) 'The industrialization of service', *Harvard Business Review*, September/October, pp.63–74.

Linder, S.B. (1970) *The Harried Leisure Class*, New York, Columbia University Press.

Reading source

Smythe (1995/1981) pp.222–8   ■ ■ ■

After Smythe's first article on this topic came out in 1977 there was considerable debate within CPEM about whether the model he had outlined was correct. Other researchers argued that it was wrong to characterise audience members as workers in their role of viewing, listening or reading. These, after all, were fundamentally different kinds of activity from the labour involved in, say, a factory. Most importantly, in terms of economic role, consumption ought to be clearly differentiated from production. Whatever the merits of these arguments the important point is that the audience-as-commodity, the concept that it is something to be bought and sold, has been a significant way of understanding the media. And as you may have reflected while doing the activity, even though it is very critical this approach is surprisingly close to the way in which commercial media make sense of the audience.

The present chapter is called 'The media's view of the audience', the focus being on the way in which media makers try to understand the audience. But as we are starting to see, CPEM does not approach the question of the audience in a neutral fashion, whereby it is assumed to consist of people who freely choose to watch, listen or read. On the contrary, for CPEM researchers the audience is constructed in and through its political economic function as a commodity or a target for advertising. The result is that, as forms of media and advertising change, so too do audiences. We can see this in the recent history of the UK press.

3.1 How advertising moulds newspapers and readerships

James Curran (1986) argues that advertising has had a major impact on the structure of UK media in the period since the introduction of commercial television in the UK in 1956. The bright new platform of ITV attracted advertising revenue away from other media, particularly the popular newspaper press, which as a consequence lost five titles in the period 1960–64. The remaining popular newspapers responded to the crisis by pushing down their advertising rates, so reducing profit margins further. In this situation the urgent need was to build circulation, which some of the papers did through increasing the space devoted to human interest stories – at the expense of hard news (a process known as 'tabloidisation'). In fact, such stories had consistently been the best liked among the readership of *all* newspapers. Yet the 'quality' papers did not go down the road of increasing human interest content because they commanded much higher advertising rates than the popular titles. The economic logic here was to build a small, upmarket readership (or audience commodity in Smythe's terms) for the expensive products advertised in their pages (see Figure 3.3). This could best be done by marking out an elite identity, with low human interest and high news content.

Figure 3.3 *Selling luxury goods to an upmarket readership: an advertisement from a UK newspaper*

Curran's closely observed account of post-Second World War UK media suggests that polarisation in the content and readership of the press is far from being a matter of reader preference as market liberals might conclude. Rather, 'tabloidisation' can be explained only by changes in the way the audience was divided up for delivery to advertisers. To the extent that knowing the audience is at stake here, this is a matter of knowing the unequal buying power of its different parts, and, in particular, the desire for cultural distinction of the wealthiest sector. To put it another way, an understanding of class, and how to exploit it, is key to the strategies of the press.

3.2 Chasing the audience: evidence from within the industry

So far in Section 3 I have been examining what might be described as the core CPEM position. In terms of methodology, it has involved a) starting with the structural-economic features of media organisations, especially the crucial importance of advertising revenue; and b) examining how trends in audience size and composition, together with shifts in media type, might confirm the hypothesis that advertising drives the media's approach to knowing, or better, to *making*, the audience.

Significantly, the findings of CPEM researchers have been confirmed in broad terms by an important piece of research that has used quite a different methodology. In the autumn and winter of 1980, Todd Gitlin (1994/1983) interviewed a series of US television network personnel, from executives to actors. On the basis of his interview material he concluded that a preoccupation with audience size was having a damaging effect on content and leading to constant rescheduling at the expense of the development of quality television. For key decision makers in the networks it was not knowledge of the audience, and its preferences, that was at stake so much as fear of advertisers. As Gitlin puts it:

> All that can be said for sure is that a single rating-point difference, sustained over the course of an entire year, could be worth $50 million or more at 1981 advertising rates; so when a show is marginal and the numbers ambiguous, it's easy for actual and anticipated advertiser pressure to make the difference.
>
> Gitlin, 1994/1983, pp.9–10

What Gitlin points to, then, is an extraordinary sensitivity to advertisers on the part of the television networks; in the audience commodity market it seems that buyers of air time are in a commanding position. Gitlin is undoubtedly in broad agreement with CPEM here. Yet in one important sense his conclusions lead away from the latter's structural-economic approach. For where CPEM argues that a kind of impersonal adjustment goes on between content, media organisation and the audience commodity in response to changing historical forces in the capitalist system, Gitlin proposes that uncertainty is crucial. It is a major impediment in the decision making of the key corporate players. What the media are confronted with is 'the problem of knowing'; and with this formulation (which Gitlin uses for a chapter title) we are squarely back to the issues of distance, mediation and uncertainty of demand that I examined in the Introduction to this chapter.

Reading 3.3 Activity

Now read the following extract from Todd Gitlin's *Inside Prime Time*, (Reading 3.3). This extract reflects on the difficulties faced by television executives in judging audience taste. Compare his analysis with Smythe's discussion of the audience commodity in Reading 3.2. What do the two extracts have to say about media power and the extent to which the audience can be comprehended by the media?

Reading 3.3

Todd Gitlin, 'Nothing succeeds like "success"'

Corporations typically evolve from entrepreneurship to bureaucracy. Defenders of this presumably iron law say that in principle what is lost in the founders' brilliance and sharpness of purpose is more than compensated for by a gain in knowledge. Hence, the multiplication of bureaucratic layers and the growth of scientific management have proceeded hand in hand. Like other giant marketing combines, the networks have come to rely on hard knowledge: the data that come from program testing, the performance of precedents, social research on popular moods, and most of all, once a show gets on the air, its performance as measured by the Nielsen ratings. In defensive and belligerent moods, executives claim the warrant of science. Yet most of them also acknowledge the limits of their data. They know that, for all their calculations, most new shows will fail to rate high enough to last into a second season. Knowing the limits, paradoxically, makes them feel knowing. Science has not triumphed. Instinct still counts for something in this unpredictable business. The premium stays on imponderables: an air of knowingness, or some ineffable quality of the person – like Fred Silverman's [a US television executive] famous 'gut' – that enables him to divine a show's chances.

There is a premium on this sort of knowingness in an industry whose business it is to cater to diffuse desires. What exactly will people 'want to watch'? The movie mogul Samuel Goldwyn once pointed out that, after all, nothing could stop people from not going to the movies. And however habit-forming television is, nothing can stop a sufficiently decisive viewer from changing channels, even turning off the set. The problem, then, is how to paralyze the will of that potentially decisive viewer; or, to put it more positively, how to keep him or her sufficiently satisfied. Though there are scientific trappings to the testing process, most network 'knowledge' is of the improvised, seat-of-the-pants variety.

For one thing, the networks fall back on certain traditional genres and styles that predate giant corporations, broadcasting, and the culture of consumer capitalism in general. What these do share with modern TV culture is the search for immediate effects. [...]

If most genres and formulas are rooted in tradition, some are more recent: for background assumptions are one thing and here-and-now television quite another. Executives know that genres become exhausted, as did the western, or seem unsuited to the small screen, like science fiction. New genres spring up, like the situation comedy, descendant of radio, which in turn drew on vaudeville sketches. Sitcoms, with their incessant skein of personal problems in a family-like setting, seem peculiarly tailored to the small screen, to its living-room locations, and to advertisers' desire for captive audiences whose commercials must be studded, like gems, in suitable settings.

But genres and traditions do not decide to buy new programs: executives do. If we think of popular taste as a liquid brew of conventional expectations, themes, and desires, held in suspension, then we may think of actual television programs as solid precipitates that suppliers and executives adapt and shape. (The suppliers – producers and studios – store old materials and devise new ones, but their resources are decisively limited by their sense of what the networks are buying.) What does this audience 'want,' they ask? The mass audience may be, say, at once alarmed about crime and admiring of stylish folk who violate the law with impunity. Executives may decide to cater to the former with a show about a high-speed, high-powered tactical police unit, or to the latter with a comedy about good ole boys who break the driving laws in the course of catching real crooks despite the incompetence and corruption of the local police. Both formulas have gotten on the air in recent years. The first, *Strike Force*, was a one-season failure; the second, *The Dukes of Hazzard*, a multiyear hit. The point is that both choices were defensible, indeed defended, with arguments about public sentiment.

> Other possible themes were also held in suspension, but didn't precipitate out because the executives didn't take a chance on them.
>
> *Reading source*
> Gitlin, 1994/1983, pp.26–30 ■ ■ ■

Gitlin turns, later in his book, to examine the Nielsen ratings and the way they are used within the television industry to inform programme development and selection. Here he points to something slightly different. It is not just that network executives are fickle when it comes to audience research: sometimes they follow the ratings slavishly, at other times they revert to 'gut instinct' about a new programme idea. More than this, the Nielsen system itself produces a skewed view of who watches. Perhaps most significantly, it under-represents minority ethnic groups and the poor. This is not the result of a conspiracy, but the effect of relatively low levels of co-operation. Households from these social groups tend not to respond to requests for participation as a 'Nielsen family'. Or if they do respond then they may well under-record (in the period of Gitlin's study, diaries were still extensively used for network audience measurement). Finally, census information, on which Neilsen samples are based, is likely to under-represent minority ethnic groups and the poor. Nielsen, as we have seen, contend that the introduction of the people meter, and their minority ethnic group ratings lists, have addressed this problem. But fundamental doubts about the accuracy of syndicated research remain.

We began this section with a critical analysis, from Smythe, of the way the media produce the audience commodity. Curran's account of UK media and advertising begins from this broad position, but then adds a historical dimension to it. Changes in media structure and consumption mean that media organisations tend to re-evaluate and repackage their audiences for delivery to advertisers in new ways. Now Gitlin has proposed that uncertainty about audience taste and insecurity about measurement together generate volatility in television scheduling. In the next section I examine an approach to media audience research that goes much further in this direction. It is highly sceptical not only about its accuracy, but indeed the very notion of a measurable audience.

4   The institutional audience: a desperate fiction?

Ien Ang's book *Desperately Seeking the Audience* caused a considerable stir in media studies when it came out in 1991. Here was a study of television that contradicted both the view from the media industries, which Ang called the 'institutional point of view', and the critical, CPEM approach. As we have seen, both of these assume there is a knowable audience, in other words a cohesive and measurable group of people engaged in the activity of attending to media texts. But for Ang this point of view is a fiction, and the more starkly so for the intensity with which it is asserted as a fact by media institutions. Significantly, Ang includes public service broadcasters and media policy makers among those subscribing to the institutional point of view. For this approach to the audience is not just a matter of economics, of the capitalist imperative to accumulate through the production of an audience commodity as CPEM suggests. Much more, Ang argues, it is an instance of 'control through knowledge' (Ang, 1991, p.7). In making this claim she draws on the work of Michel Foucault.

Some readers will have already encountered this important cultural historian and theorist. One of his main ideas is that knowledge constitutes truth. Instead of there being a single truth that may be found *by means* of thinking, enquiring, researching, and so on, truth is encapsulated *in* these same knowledge tools. Truth is no more, or less, than an effect of knowledge. What is more, on the other side of the coin of knowledge we find power. This is because power arises from the way organised systems of knowledge fix things and give them a certain order. We can see this most clearly in the modern bureaucratic structures of the military, the various arms of the civil state such as the judicial system or education, and of course private corporations.

For Ang, Foucault's approach to power–knowledge provides the perfect explanatory framework for thinking about how the television institution summons up an audience through its procedures of planning and measuring. And there is a further aspect of Foucault's work that she employs. In *Discipline and Punish* Foucault (1979) charted the birth of the modern prison. A key aspect of the prison was surveillance, the fact that prisoners could be seen by their jailors at will, through spy-holes, in the prison yard, and so on. This principle of control through visibility was expressed most succinctly, according to Foucault, in the Panopticon, a model prison sketched out by the utilitarian philosopher, Jeremy Bentham, at the end of the eighteenth century. Here warders were to be stationed in a central tower with the cells of the jail arrayed in a circle around it. Shielded by venetian blinds the inspectors of the Panopticon could see, but were themselves invisible to, the prisoners.

Now read the following extract from Ien Ang's book, *Desperately Seeking the Audience* (Reading 3.4). This extract describes some of the features that television audience measurement shares with Bentham's Panopticon as well as differences between them. Try to identify what these common features are. Then compare her Foucauldian approach with the institutional view (the media's view) of audience research, focusing on the status of knowledge in each. To what extent do Ang and the media institutions consider there is an 'actual' audience?

Ien Ang, 'Revolt of the viewer?'

I am reminded of these insights of Foucault in trying to make sense of the developments in audience measurement practices that I have been discussing here. In fact, the principles of panopticism are central to the technological operation of audience measurement: its core mechanism, and ultimate ambition, is control through visibility. Audience measurement too is a form of examination: its aim is to put television viewers under constant scrutiny, to describe their behaviour so as to turn them into suitable objects in and for industry practices, to judge their viewing habits in terms of their productivity for advertisers and broadcasters alike. What audience measurement accomplishes is the production of a discourse which 'formalizes' and reduces the viewer into a calculable audience member, someone whose behaviour can be objectively determined and neatly categorized. As we have seen, this discursive streamlining of 'television audience' is extremely useful for the industry: it effectuates a comforting sense of predictability and controllability in an uncertain environment.

However, it would be misleading to see audience measurement as a regular instance of the disciplinary arrangements Foucault talks about. Television viewers cannot be subjected to officially sanctioned disciplinary control such as is the case with schoolchildren or prisoners. In these institutions disciplinary techniques are aimed at transforming people through punishment, through training and correction. The living room however is emphatically not a classroom or a private cell, nor is television a 'carceral' institution. After all, watching television takes place in the context of domestic leisure, under the banner of the hedonism of consumer society, in which the idea of audience freedom forms a prominent ideological value.[1] Therefore the commercial television industry cannot have the power to effectuate the conversion of viewers into what Foucault (1979) has termed 'docile bodies', implying total behavioural control over them – that is, the ability to force them to adopt the 'ideal' viewing behaviour (for example, watch all the commercials attentively).[2]

This problem – that is, the problem that viewers are not prisoners but 'free' consumers – accounts for the limits of audience measurement as a practice of control. Indeed, it would even be ideologically impossible to officially present it as a practice of control: instead it is called, as we have seen, a practice of creating 'feedback'. The importance given to methodological accuracy and objectivity in discussions about audience measurement may be understood against this background: emphasizing that audience measurement is a matter of research not control increases its credibility and legitimacy and reduces distrust against it. All this amounts to the fact that audience measurement can only be an indirect means of disciplining the television audience: it is through symbolic, not literal objectification and subjection that ratings discourse, by streamlining 'television audience', performs its controlling function. It does not effect the actual discipline of television viewers, it only conjures it up in its imagination. This leads to a fundamental contradiction in the very motif of audience measurement. Just as the disciplinary technologies described by Foucault, ratings services put viewers under constant examination. But contrary to what happens, for example, in the prison, the visibility of people-watching-television achieved by audience measurement is not linked up with the organization of direct behavioural control: observation and regulation of bodies do not go together here. In other words, audience measurement is an incomplete panoptic arrangement: the power/knowledge linkage is, in a sense, rather precarious. This does not mean that there is no power and control involved in the set-up of audience measurement; it does mean, however, that the production of ever more refined knowledge as such becomes a rather autonomous pursuit: stripped of a direct material effect on its object of scrutiny, audience measurement is carried out in the tacit belief that the production of knowledge as such – that is, the construction of a streamlined map of 'television audience' – must somehow automatically lead to control over actual audiences. To put it in a different way, even if audience measurement cannot be seen as a true panoptic technology, panopticism is inscribed in it insofar as the whole project is inspired by the ideal of such a form of control, and driven by the constant theoretical and practical search for the best mechanisms to do so. We will see, however, that the project has quite contradictory effects, not at all uniformly leading to the desired increased control.

To be sure, the technologies of audience measurement – meter, diary, telephone interview, people meter – do involve actual entry in the living rooms of (a small number of) actual viewers, in order to put them under constant examination. These technologies indicate that audience measurement is basically an ingenious means for the industry to obliquely penetrate people's private spaces, in order to make 'visible', in a roundabout way, what would otherwise take place out of sight (and therefore beyond control). But, unfortunately for the industry, the ratings firms can only incorporate families and households in their samples (and intrude in their homes) when they agree to it. While people's freedom to reject their subjection to surveillance is something to be respected in a free society, it is also unwittingly perceived as an unfortunate circumstance, an inconvenience: think of the concern about 'the non co-operation problem', the suspense around 'compliance rates'.

The problem has become all the more pronounced with the launch of the people meter technology. The futuristic passive people meter, in particular, comes dangerously close to a literal materialization of panoptic mechanisms: with the (passive) people meter, the process of subjection to the examining apparatus is becoming all too obvious. And indeed, this theme is well reflected in the public controversy around the people meter. With the introduction of the people meter, audience measurement is becoming too explicit and palpable an instance of monitoring viewers. Thus, the people meter has repetitiously been given a bad press as a 'manifestation of Big Brother': observers note 'the new technology's spooky Orwellian overtones' (Waters and Uehling, 1985) (is it mere coincidence that public debate on the people meter started in 1984?), while one industry official expressed his personal doubts about the passive people meter as follows: 'My concern is more from the big-brother standpoint. If somehow, somewhere a computer knows this massive weight is a 53 year-old male, that scares me. What else does it know about me?' (in *Broadcasting* 5 January 1987: 63).

But this kind of moral concern about the people meter, cast as it is in the liberal discourse of intrusion of privacy, overlooks the less conspicuously obtrusive, but more structural 'rationality' of the very practice of audience measurement. Not only the people meter, but all audience measurement technologies in principle depend on the propriety of having people submit themselves to permanent monitoring. From this point of view, the people meter is not a qualitative break, but merely represents one more step in the technological sophistication of the enterprise; the old setmeter and the paper-and-pencil diary are simply somewhat more 'primitive' devices ('little big brothers' as it were) whose operation is similarly based upon the principle of control through visibility.[3]

Notes

1 However, the idea of the living room as a kind of classroom does play a role in the reformist context of public service broadcasting [...]

2 Besides, in the competitive world of the television industry there cannot possibly be a consensus about what 'ideal' viewing habits are: what is 'ideal' for (one of) the networks may be not so 'ideal' for the advertisers, or for the cable companies, and so on.

3 That anxiety over the Big Brother threat should have become particularly prominent in relation to the people meter, may be explained by the system's greater emphasis on observation of the individual human body, the sacred site of self in Western culture.

References

Foucault, M. (1979) *Discipline and Punish: The Birth of the Prison*, London, Penguin.

Waters, H. and Uehling, M. (1985) 'Tuning in on the viewer', *Newsweek*, 4 March.

Reading source

Ang, 1991, pp.86–8 ■ ■ ■

Ang's assessment of audience research in Reading 3.4 is that it represents a form of surveillance. Just as in the case of prisoners in the Panopticon, the television audience is systematically watched. The object is to make those surveyed into 'calculable' objects, controllable because they have been measured. Yet, as you may already have noticed, Ang is keen to qualify how effective this process is. In fact many of the pages of *Desperately Seeking the Audience* are devoted to showing that research fails quite comprehensively to apprehend the audience. The gap between the institutional point of view and the actual behaviour of audiences is huge. Ang points to several specific reasons as well as some more general principles. To begin with there are problems of method. Responding to research questions is irksome and depends on memory, a human faculty that is always frail and given to error. Of course, the industry acknowledges this as we have seen: the introduction of the people meter was intended precisely to overcome the reliance of the diary system on an inherently weak memory. Yet the people meter also depends on agency, the voluntary participation of audience members. Pressing a button on and off when one begins, and also when one ceases, to watch is a banal yet difficult task to carry out if it is to be done scrupulously. Quite apart from forgetting or not bothering to do it, one may mischievously misrepresent one's viewing (Ang, 1991, pp.80–3). In addition, new forms of television viewing, particularly cable and the VCR, increase the complexity and variability of watching television. 'Zipping' and 'zapping' (respectively, using the video and switching through channels) (see Figure 3.4) make recording of audience activity more problematic in that these activities require extra work from research respondents. As a rule, Ang observes, the more onerous and complex the task, the poorer the quality of reporting (Ang, 1991, pp.73–7).

In fact this principle extends to *all* kinds of audience research. Magazine readership, for example, is notoriously difficult to gauge.

Figure 3.4 *Remote controls, developed in the 1960s, but only widely available from the 1980s, have made zapping an integral part of the television experience*

4.1 New technologies: new problems of measurement and control

Ang was writing before the advent of the internet. But in the case of the Web the multiplicity of channels (there are millions of websites), and the high degree of interactivity make measurement even more complicated. Early internet research used the index of the 'hit'. Yet counting clicks on a site says nothing about the quality of use, nor the identity of the user. This matters because most commercial websites are advertising funded, and so there is the same imperative to measure audience-hood that we find in television. As a result, since the end of the 1990s, measurement on a similar model has been introduced, with people meter-style software being installed on PCs used by research participants. The trouble is that this technological fix cannot obviate a much larger problem, namely how to ensure a big enough sample to capture use of the full range of internet sites. Currently, the major measurement firms have a sample frame of 70,000 people. Yet despite the enormous scale of this research there is widespread scepticism about its effectiveness – there are certainly many sites whose use is never registered (Napoli, 2003, pp.91–2).

To return to Ang, what is interesting is that she already anticipates this scenario in 1991. It leads into the final strand of her argument, which I will examine here. If new surveillance technology is developed to match new kinds of media use, there may well be a self-defeating logic at work. As Ang puts it:

> The more it sees, the less it can to get grips with what it sees, as it were. The calculable audience member tends to dissipate before the ever more sensitive microscope of audience measurement, and increasingly regains his or her status of active subject. Audience measurement, in short, is an example of how the practice of panoptic examination, when severed from the attendant power of disciplining behaviour, turns out to have a contradictory outcome: rather than facilitating control it makes it more difficult!
>
> Ang, 1991, p.95

So, is there really an audience at all? In her conclusion, Ang suggests that watching television is 'a complex and dynamic cultural process, fully integrated in the messiness of everyday life' (Ang, 1991, p.160). David Morley (1990) echoes this point when he suggests that the mere fact of having a television switched on does not necessarily indicate audience-hood. The variability in degree of attention, type of watching and empathy with the programme found both in and between households makes any notion of a unitary audience problematic. The next activity addresses this issue by asking you to reflect on your own experience. It might be helpful to move away from television, and think about another, even more ubiquitous, medium: radio.

Activity 3.3

Do you ever think of yourself as a member of the radio audience? Consider your own, your friends' or your family's radio listening – and not just the listening, but what you are doing all the time the radio is on. To what extent do you and the people you know become an 'audience'? ■ ■ ■

Of course some listeners are very attentive and loyal to 'their' radio station, more so than with television. Conversely, others are casual, inattentive or occasional listeners. But whatever answers you came up with in response to the questions in Activity 3.3, perhaps the key point to note is that simply asking such questions goes against the grain of the institutional point of view, which can be described as a confident belief in the given-ness of the audience. For whether or not there can be said to be one, media organisations always insist that there is a knowable body of people who are all attending to the media in a more or less coherent way. Indeed, the media depend for their very existence on such an assertion.

In the next section I examine some implications of this contradiction and in particular the possibility that it is becoming more acute, that is to say the diffuseness of audiences may be increasing, even as marketing and research divisions in the media treat audiences more and more as though they were concrete entities that can be weighed, measured and targeted.

5 Knowing the audience: continuity, change and the question of power

With the introduction of new media technologies, marketing strategies and increasing deregulation, the media have undoubtedly undergone significant change in the last thirty years or so. What is more, behind these shifts lie two much bigger developments. The first is the rise of neo-liberalism, that set of ideas that legitimates private ownership and the market, and that was launched on the world stage with the arrival of the Thatcher and Reagan administrations at the turn of the 1970s. Second, and assisted by neo-liberal ideas and policy, we encounter increasing conglomeration and concentration of media ownership in the hands of a small number of large corporations with diverse media holdings (Hesmondhalgh, 2002). The question is, though, how significant have these changes been for the way in which the media approach the audience?

Cinema provides an interesting case study. Justin Wyatt (1994) argues that there has been a shift towards the 'high concept' film since the 1970s. Such films are based on a simple idea that can be easily 'pitched' and comprehensively market tested. The result, he suggests, is increasing formularisation. For Miller et al. (2001) too, more intensive 'surveillance' of the film audience in the contemporary period feeds into tighter control of creative decision making by marketing divisions. Pre-testing and the use of telephone research of audiences for newly released films play a critical role. Even more significantly, these are now just one aspect of a larger trend towards consumer surveillance, a trend fed by conglomeration. As Miller et al. put it, market research facilitates:

> an integrated marketing concept, one that includes all the major exhibition windows (theatrical release, home video, pay-per-view TV, national cable and satellite television, network television, local cable and broadcast television and the internet) plus recorded music and publishing, as well as tie-in merchandising and cross promotions with retailers, restaurants and any other entertainment or leisure industry promotion.
>
> Miller et al., 2001, p.191

If this list, and the range of media products that it covers, does not seem large enough, the writers also point to the international dimension of contemporary film marketing. The growth of tie-ins, multiple formats and the measured audiences on which these rely, is now occurring on a global basis. Hollywood surveys the audience everywhere.

All of this seems, on the face of it, to represent something new: not the making of a single audience commodity as in the case of traditional broadcast television, but the production of multiple commodities engaged in the mutual constitution of one another. In effect, film exhibition delivers an audience for video, merchandising promotes CD soundtrack sales – the chain of reciprocal commodification goes on and on. As for research, rather than being commissioned by each media sector a comprehensive, interlocking approach is now taken to knowing the audience. This is a quantitative leap forward that is beginning to look like a qualitative one.

However, there is evidence to suggest that the film industry has carried out comprehensive marketing and audience research, and acted upon it in order to shape creative decisions, from the earliest days of Hollywood. Gerben Bakker (2003) traces how previewing became a key part of Hollywood marketing from the 1920s. For example, an important scene in *King Kong* (1933) was reshot after a preview audience reacted in disgust to images of the great ape's pursuers being attacked by huge insects and snakes. Beyond previewing, the industry has been using branding techniques, with stars rendered as 'internal' commodities within films, over many years. From the 1930s the major studios tracked the success and failure of films across each season's releases in a systematic way using sales data. This information would be used to indicate whether the stars contracted to each company should be retained or dropped. Finally, from the 1940s detailed research into the popularity of both film stars and formats was carried out. On the basis of the research data, winning combinations of stars were devised in order to maximise audience appeal for big-budget films.

It seems, then, that the application of audience research in order to format films and maximise star-value is nothing new. What is significant, however, is that such practices have increased in scale and complexity in recent years. Perhaps most important of all, integrated marketing and audience research now serves the production of films and derivative products *across* media owned by giant communication conglomerates.

These developments raise questions about media power, which I noted at the beginning of the chapter, with a particular urgency. Are the media industries gaining more power over the audience through their increasing concentration on marketing and audience research? Or should we read these innovations as a sign of greater responsiveness to an audience whose interests are now better understood and served than ever before? These are complex questions and we need to avoid simplistic responses. For one thing, as I have already noted, there are some contradictory indications. In the case of cinema, market research has served the expansion of a mass market for films across different media, and based on derivative products. With magazines, on the other hand, we encounter increasing segmentation and the shaking out of older titles based on broad readerships. The UK popular music press provides a case in point.

In the mid 1970s three weekly music magazines, the so-called 'inkies', dominated the market. *New Musical Express* (*NME*), *Melody Maker* and *Sounds* were all owned by the publisher IPC, and all offered a broadly similar mix of features and reviews about rock music together with a certain amount of youth-oriented advertising. As a journalist for the *NME* Mick Farren (see Figure 3.5) was, by his own account (2001), given a large degree of freedom to choose both topic and approach in his writing. In this environment understanding the audience was very much a matter for journalists; market research would have been anathema. For, above all, to know your readers meant understanding (and sometimes lampooning) a rock, subcultural constituency to which you yourself belonged.

By the mid 1980s the range of magazines had already been expanding for several years: a bi-weekly *Smash Hits* sold to a teenage, pop-fan readership in huge quantities (up to 800,000), while the relatively small but vigorous weekly, *Kerrang!*, served aficionados of heavy metal. Then in 1986 the glossy monthly, *Q*, was launched to cater for an older generation of rock fans. It carried a considerable number of high-revenue advertisements. But the trend towards segmentation really accelerated in the 1990s with the failure of some rock titles, including the venerable *Sounds*, the emergence of a new dance music magazine niche, and the launch of a large circulation pop glossy from the BBC, *Top of the Pops*. By the mid 2000s the rock magazine format, which had appeared to be such a permanent fixture in the 1970s, had been utterly transformed. Only the *NME* survived from the earlier period – and in a glossy, tabloid format.

At a general level these changes can be explained by the fact that music magazines are now sold to quite distinct readerships. Undoubtedly this reflects the fragmentation of what has been called 'heartland rock'; music consumption is itself organised into distinct communities of taste these days. But the new structure also has to do with a new attention to marketing and reader research in the multimedia conglomerates that control consumer magazines. Eamonn Forde describes this as 'a dual movement towards niche orientation and title branding' (Forde, 2003, p.119). On the one hand small readerships with a narrow consumer profile are targeted. Advertising contributed 36 per cent to net consumer magazine revenue at the end of the 1990s, and advertisers have

Figure 3.5 *Mick Farren, interviewing musicians (and eschewing audience research)*
Source: *Give the Anarchist a Cigarette*, Farren, 2002

increasingly demanded 'efficient' platforms that deliver readers with just the right lifestyle for their products. On the other hand, the title brand has been extended laterally in a similar way to that which we saw in film. So, the *NME* now has a website, a sponsored annual awards ceremony (with coverage on television), and a radio station delivered by digital broadcast and the internet. Notionally, the same audience will attend to, or buy into, the brand across all the platforms.

There is a further aspect to these developments. Journalists are no longer representatives of their readership in the way in which they were at least nominally in the 1970s. Rather, there is a co-ordinated system of planning and control across the 'portfolio' of magazines owned by a publisher. The result, as Forde explains, is that:

> strategic long-term planning is conducted between the publishers and all the editors in the portfolio to avoid inter-title cannibalism and to ensure that each title 'inherits' readers from the title before it in the chain and encourage readers to 'graduate' to the next title in the chain. This filters down into each individual newsroom, affecting in particular ways how each of the section editors operates and how both their individual and collective goals are defined and realised.
>
> Forde, 2003, p.128

What Forde observes in the music press typifies something that is happening right across the media. As niche marketing, branding and portfolio management have taken off, so too the autonomy of creative workers has declined. Journalists are becoming less able to conceive of their readers as a public whom they might address in a relatively direct fashion (see **Herbert, 2005**). Instead, their decisions about what to write and for whom are being determined by strategic decisions made at a high level within large, multimedia publishing organisations. Increasingly, then, as a creative worker you are *told* how to know your audience.

Activity 3.4

Think about other kinds of work in the media at the creative or production stage. You might want to consult Chapter 4 in this book, or look at published accounts by musicians, actors, directors, etc. Has creative autonomy been undermined by new forms of knowing the audience; if so, does this apply to all media sectors, and are there other tendencies at work? ■ ■ ■

In Section 5 I have charted the ways in which knowing the audience has changed, yet in other respects remained stable, in the media since the 1970s. These are summarised in Table 3.3.

Table 3.3 Continuity and change in media audiences since the 1970s

Aspects of media audience research	Continuity/Change
Pre-testing and audience research influence product design	Continuity; more of the same
Development of rational research techniques designed to yield positive knowledge of audiences	Continuity, but techniques now used in new media with more channels (the internet is the strongest example)
Mass audiences	Continuity, but mass audiences are now channelled towards derivative products (as in the case of film, for example)
Segmentation of audiences	More segmentation, both within and across media
Audience commodity is delivered to advertisers	Continuity, but also the development of complex audience commodities, where each helps to build another within the brand
Media's image of the audience is generated by media professionals and creative workers	Increasingly, a new, corporate image of the audience is imposed on creative workers

6 Conclusion

I began the chapter by analysing that tension between knowledge and uncertainty about the audience that seems to be so characteristic of mediated communication. In an important sense, the three main approaches that I then examined situate themselves along a line between these poles of knowledge and uncertainty.

The position of the industry can be characterised as one of confident assurance that audience research works. Not only does it provide useful information, which reduces uncertainty and therefore waste, it also enables the funding of media production through advertising. Good knowledge makes for audience satisfaction, and a free lunch as well. For the critical political economy of the media (CPEM) position, the way in which media organisations know the audience is a matter of control and exploitation. The audience is produced (the work is done by its own members according to Smythe) and sold on to advertisers. There is not much uncertainty here. However, some researchers close to CPEM have shown that audience commodities are given to change (Curran), or else audience awareness produces a state of permanent volatility within media organisations (Gitlin). Lastly, Ang and Morley point to the chronic failure of the media to know the audience. In their messy complexity, audiences resist measurement and classification.

As for the question of change, which I examined in Section 5, there clearly is some, but it is difficult to assess its extent and significance. It does seem reasonable to conclude, however, that, in as much as large corporations are systematically marketing symbolic products across a whole range of media assets, creative workers and audiences have less power and less ability to shape the form and quality of their relationship.

Answer to activity

Activity Answer 3.2

You need to multiply the number of households by 100, and divide the result by the share figure. ▪ ▪ ▪

Further reading

Ettema, J. and Whitney, D. (1994) (eds) *Audience Making: How the Media Create the Audience*, Thousand Oaks, CA, Sage. A useful collection. There are chapters here on a number of different media as well as on various aspects of the media–audience relationship. Generally, as the title suggests, the argument is that media construct the audience rather than simply responding to it.

Napoli, P. (2003) *Audience Economics: Media Institutions and the Audience Marketplace*, New York, Columbia University Press. This is a very thorough survey of media audience research in the USA with a special focus on television. Napoli makes some interesting observations about key issues such as uncertainty and the nature of the audience commodity.

Picard, R. (2002) 'Research note: assessing audience performance of public service broadcasters', *European Journal of Communication*, vol.17, no.2, pp.227–35. Using audience research data collected by public service broadcasters across Europe, this essay argues that PSB organisations are holding their own in terms of share in the increasingly competitive environment of multi-channel television. How long this conclusion will still be valid is an open question, but the essay is interesting, apart from anything else, for its comparative analysis of audience data.

Screen Digest, Global Media Intelligence. Published on a monthly basis, *Screen Digest* provides up-to-date media industry research from around the world with a special emphasis on audiences and markets. It is a trade journal, and the analysis is therefore oriented towards the media industries. Nonetheless, *Screen Digest* has very useful and detailed information on specific sectors.

Turow, J. (1998) *Breaking Up America: Advertisers and the New Media World*, Chicago, IL, Chicago University Press. Turow describes the way in which the advertising and media industries have collaborated in producing niche markets and fragmented audiences since the mid-1970s. The book is critical of this trend and suggests some negative implications that follow from it for US culture.

References

Ang, I. (1991) *Desperately Seeking the Audience*, London, Routledge.

Audience Research and Development (2004) 'Model audience groups', Audience Research and Development, http://www.ar-d.com/mag.html (accessed 1 February 2004).

Bakker, G. (2003) 'Building knowledge about the consumer: the emergence of market research in the motion picture industry', *Business History*, vol.45, no.1, pp.101–27.

Blumer, H. (1966) 'The mass, the public, and public opinion' in Berelson, B. and Janowitz, M. (eds) *Reader in Public Opinion and Communication*, New York, Free Press.

Caves, R. (2001) *Creative Industries: Contracts Between Art and Commerce*, Cambridge, MA, Harvard University Press.

Curran, J. (1986) 'The impact of advertising on the British mass media' in Collins, R., Curran, J., Sparks, C., Garnham, N., Scannell, P. and Schlesinger, P. (eds) *Media, Culture and Society: A Critical Reader*, London, Sage.

Farren, M. (2001) *Give the Anarchist a Cigarette*, London, Jonathan Cape.

Forde, E. (2003) 'Journalists with a difference: producing music journalism' in Cottle, S. (ed.) *Media Organization and Production*, London, Sage.

Foucault, M. (1979) *Discipline and Punish: The Birth of the Prison*, London, Penguin.

Garnham, N. (1990) 'Contribution to a political economy of mass communication' in *Capitalism and Communication: Global Culture and the Economics of Information*, London, Sage.

Gillespie, M. (2005) 'Television, drama and audience ethnography' in Gillespie, M. (ed.) *Media Audiences*, Maidenhead, Open University Press/The Open University (Book 2 in this series).

Gitlin, T. (1994/1983) *Inside Prime Time* (2nd edn), London, Routledge.

Greene, K. (2000) 'TV's test pilots', *Broadcasting and Cable*, 17 July, p.52.

Herbert, D. (2005) 'Media publics, culture and democracy' in Gillespie, M. (ed.) *Media Audiences*, Maidenhead, Open University Press/The Open University (Book 2 in this series).

Hesmondhalgh, D. (2002) *The Cultural Industries*, London, Sage.

Hesmondhalgh, D. (2005) 'Producing celebrity' in Evans, J. and Hesmondhalgh, D. (eds) *Understanding Media: Inside Celebrity*, Maidenhead, Open University Press/The Open University (Book 1 in this series).

Miller, P. (1994) 'Made-to-order and standardized audiences: forms of reality in audience measurement' in Ettema, J. and Whitney, D. (eds) *Audience Making: How the Media Create the Audience*, Thousand Oaks, CA, Sage.

Miller, T., Govill, N., McMurria, J. and Maxwell, R. (2001) *Global Hollywood*, London, BFI Publishing.

Morley, D. (1990) 'Beyond the ratings: the politics of audience research' in Willis, J. and Wollen, T. (eds) *The Neglected Audience*, London, BFI Publishing.

Napoli, P. (2003) *Audience Economics: Media Institutions and the Audience Marketplace*, New York, Columbia University Press.

Negus, K. (1999) *Music Genres and Corporate Cultures*, London, Routledge.

Nielsen Media Research (2004) *Measuring Through Representative Samples*, Nielsen Media Research, http://www.nielsenmedia.com/ethnicmeasure/sampling.html (accessed 1 February 2004).

Smythe, D. (1995/1981) 'On the audience commodity and its work' in Boyd-Barrett, O. and Newbold, C. (eds) *Approaches to Media: A Reader*, London, Arnold.

Thompson, J. (1995) *The Media and Modernity*, Stanford, CA, Stanford University Press.

Wyatt, J. (1994) *High Concept Movies and Marketing in Hollywood*, Austin, TX, University of Texas Press.

Working in the media

Chapter 4

Gillian Ursell

Contents

1 Introduction

In May 2004, controversy surrounded the film *Fahrenheit 9/11*, a scathing documentary critique of US President George W. Bush and of the 2003 invasion of Iraq. The film had been produced by Disney's subsidiary Miramax, but as its cinema release approached in the USA, it emerged that the Disney Corporation had refused to distribute it. The public and media following of the film's writer and director, Michael Moore, was of such a scale that alternative distributors were soon found; indeed, the altercation between Moore and Disney contributed to the publicity of the film, and it became a significant hit in cinemas and when released on DVD. Nevertheless, the conflict over the film had a familiar feel: media workers locked in battle with media businesses.

Behind every Michael Moore there are a hundred others, working as it were 'backstage' (see Figure 4.1), who are not in a position to attract public and media attention to the same extent as Moore. Some of these are creative workers, some work on the more humdrum, technical aspects of media. What they have in common is that they try to earn a living through media production. How should we view these backstage media workers? What are we to make of the possible conflicts between what media employers demand of them, and what they, the workers, want to achieve in media production? These questions are explored in this chapter.

Figure 4.1 *Michael Moore and his co-workers, during the production of* Roger and Me *(USA, dir. Moore, 1989)*
Source: Ronald Grant Archive

Chapter 2 has already explored issues concerning the 'autonomy' or otherwise of those who work in media organisations, and surveyed a number of key studies of power and autonomy in relation to the texts produced. Here the focus is more on media work itself (rather than on textual outcomes) and on how such work might be understood.

The chapter outlines four approaches to media work, as follows:

- media workers as an economic resource (Section 2);
- media workers as exploited under capitalism (Section 3);
- media workers as professionals (Section 4);
- media workers, identity and discourse (Section 5).

The first two approaches share a focus on the media worker as an employee of a profit-seeking industry or company. The first sees media workers as a factor of production, to be employed and deployed at the employer's will and for the employer's purposes. It does not portray the relationship of employer to employee as one of power, however. This is because in essence it construes the individual worker as an object to be managed, rather than as a subject with a mind of his or her own. The second approach is very different from this 'economic' perspective. This is the *labour process* approach. It developed from the idea, particularly associated with the US writer Harry Braverman (1920–1976), that the capitalist search for ever-higher labour productivity means that workers will increasingly become degraded and deskilled at work.

The third approach is again very different. It does not rely on any reference to capitalism or economic logic but, rather, is sociological in its analysis. It looks at media workers – especially journalists – as professionals, collectively organising to ensure that their work adheres to certain values and standards deemed by the profession to be socially desirable. This view portrays the professional worker as a member of an occupational group that, by virtue of its expert contributions and services, can expect to enjoy a high degree of autonomy in the workplace. But this autonomy has nonetheless to be won: it cannot be taken for granted that the employer (or other significant parties) will concede it. We need therefore to explore 'media professionalism' on a case-by-case basis.

The fourth approach derives from the work of the French cultural historian and social theorist Michel Foucault (see Chapter 3). It sees the individual as actively involved in selecting and enacting an identity (or even, experimenting with various identities) in a range of social contexts, one of which is likely to be work. The identity achieved, though, is not understood as an expression of individual autonomy, even if that is how the individual feels it to be. Rather, this approach argues, we should recognise that the range of possible identities is socially made: it is social 'discourse' that determines what identities are available. As we will see, this approach has some interesting perspectives to offer on media work and on the relationship of media work to modern forms of social identity.

The overall aim is to find a set of approaches that will help us understand media work. In order to do so, the chapter compares the approaches and assesses the extent to which they are useful in forming such an understanding.

2 Media workers as an economic resource: 'flexibility'

Many debates about how to maximise business efficiency have turned on questions of how to employ and deploy workers so as to increase their productivity. One important answer to this question has centred around the concept of 'flexibility'. Atkinson (1984), for example, identified three distinct management techniques for securing greater flexibility from workers in 'the flexible firm', namely:

- numerical/temporal flexibility: the numbers of people employed and the numbers of hours worked are varied according to the needs of company operations;
- functional flexibility: the type and range of tasks undertaken by any one worker are broad – they are skilled generalists rather than skilled specialists or lower-skilled workers;
- pay flexibility: workers' earnings should be open to recurrent negotiation, often on an individual-by-individual and/or project-by-project basis.

These techniques are widely used by modern employers in pursuit of enhanced efficiency – as defined by lower production costs and shorter reaction times in reorganising production arrangements to meet changes in demand for whatever product is being made. But we need to remind ourselves that the 'flexible worker' is a goal of the employers, rather than of the workers themselves. It is built on the view of the worker as first and foremost an economic resource. The individual worker is significant to the firm only in terms of his or her capacity to contribute to productivity and thence to profitability. In the theorisation of the model, the worker is not seen to make any contribution beyond that which is necessary to the employer.

A related but different account of flexibility is to be found in the work of US management theorists Piore and Sabel (1984). These writers proposed that the late twentieth century had witnessed a radical transformation from large bureaucratised companies with permanent workforces to *flexibly specialised* networks – groups made up of specialist small units of flexible workers, independent and self-managing. They anticipated that such substantial restructuring would spread throughout advanced economies and would herald a new kind of society, built upon a republic of independent, self-directing smallholders co-operating with each other for reasons of mutual self-interest; and they welcomed such change.

How do these ideas apply to the media and to media work? The characteristics of the flexible firm identified by Atkinson certainly seem to describe the techniques of the major employers in the North American and UK film industries and broadcasting in recent decades. And the pursuit of greater production and worker flexibility has certainly characterised many media industries – especially film, television, radio, new media and publishing. Indeed, some have claimed that Hollywood was the very first industry to move towards flexible specialisation (Christopherson and Storper, 1989), a claim that has been contested by, among others, Aksoy and Robins (1992). The move towards flexibility has meant that, in certain industries and organisations, fewer permanent members of staff have been employed and more use has been made of freelance and casualised staff. For example, in UK broadcasting between 1987 and 1994, the numbers permanently employed at the BBC dropped from 30,000 to 21,000, while in the ITV companies, the numbers dropped from 16,500 to 9,500 (Ursell, 1998). At the same time, the reliance of these employers on freelance workers rose, from roughly 33 per cent to over 50 per cent.

Let us now look in more detail at the idea of flexibility in broadcasting. In Reading 4.1, taken from an article by Barnatt and Starkey (1994), you will find an analysis of the restructuring of UK broadcasting towards greater flexibility. Barnatt and Starkey are here attempting to account for changes in UK television production that were substantially conditioned by government interventions. The policies of the UK Conservative government in the 1980s consistently favoured a free-market approach to the economy. This translated into the privatisation of major public services and the exposure of UK broadcasting to much greater competition, involving greatly increased risk and uncertainty. The broadcasters' coping strategies included substantial changes in work and employment, and it is this action that Barnatt and Starkey account for in terms of flexibility.

Reading 4.1 Activity

Now read the following extract from Christopher Barnatt and Kenneth Starkey's article 'The emergence of flexible networks in the UK television industry' (Reading 4.1). As you read this piece, consider the following questions:

- Against what type of corporate structure are Barnatt and Starkey contrasting these new flexibly structured production arrangements?
- Are the authors treating increased flexibility as a good thing? Do they pay sufficient attention to how workers are experiencing the changes?

Reading 4.1

Christopher Barnatt and Kenneth Starkey, 'The emergence of flexible networks in the UK television industry'

Over the last decade, the UK TV industry has become irrevocably embroiled in an ongoing process of structural transformation. In terms of both broadcast-hours output and new medias of consumer supply, expansion has been rapid, with the launch of breakfast television and Channel 4, the emergence of satellite and cable networks, and the growth of the domestic video sales and rental market. The increasingly diluted production revenues that have resulted, however, coupled with governmental pressure for change, and increasing numbers of now viable competitors, have forced the old, high-cost bureaucracies into new modes of operation. A new model of flexible organization has subsequently emerged in both the BBC and ITV that conforms closely to the flexible firm model [...]

TV production is increasingly being carried out by networks of agents (creative artists and technicians under contract to a producer or TV company), and not, as in the past, by rigid, bureaucratic corporates sourcing programmes almost exclusively from internal facilities. Indeed the BBC itself notes that the once 'high-cost' industry is now:

> characterised by increasing flexibility of employment practices and conditions, use of freelance and contracted staff ... (and the) ... growing use of externally supplied contractual services at all levels.
>
> BBC, 1992, p.12

[...]

Employment in TV covers a wide range of skills and contractual structures. The majority of employees are highly educated, many being technicians dealing with complex technologies. Others are involved with administration and finance, some are performing artists, and a few people execute 'blue collar' tasks – moving scenery, for example. The industry boasts a very high proportion of freelance personnel, and also a high number of agents and agencies employed by such individuals to gain them employment. A variety of trade unions are involved, and over the years a vast web of inter-related agreements bounding activities of both employers and employees has been spun. With the decline of the TV duopoly in production resource control, the power of such agreements is now faltering, especially because of the small size of most new production concerns. In 1989, for example, Channel 4 commissioned programmes from 526 production companies – only 28 of whom supplied material worth over £1 million. The growing array of very small independent companies within the industry, many formed on a production-by-production basis, means that 'security of tenure' for personnel is becoming scarcer.

Employment contracts for creative artists have traditionally often been of a very short-term nature, covering a period of perhaps only a few weeks, days or even hours, whereas the technicians, operators and staff production personnel employed by the BBC and ITV franchise holders were employed on a permanent basis. This, however, is rapidly changing. Thousands of permanent jobs have been lost within the BBC and big ITV companies in recent years, and new staff are likely to be employed on a contractual basis spanning anything from 3 months to 3 years. New flexible organizational networks are predicated upon the creation of four distinct groups of flexible agents: performing artists, specialist freelancers, facilities houses and contract services. These groups will form the network nodes around a production core and may be either internal or external in nature.

[...]

Figure 4.2 depicts a TV production structure whereby a single producer manages a production team, coordinating [a] flexible and dynamic resource structure in order to create programme output. This clearly represents production structuring at the *programme* level – illustrating, for example, the network created by an independent producer in fulfilling a commission for a publisher-broadcaster, or a contractual network created by allowing BBC producers control over their budgets as under *Producer Choice*. The major difference from the flexible firm [model] is that the production core of the flexible firm encompasses a number of in-house units. In Figure 4.2, the production core has been stripped down to its bare essentials and is single-project based. One can also envisage such networks as increasingly external to the broadcasting companies, with independent producers banding together and gaining commissions to produce programmes.

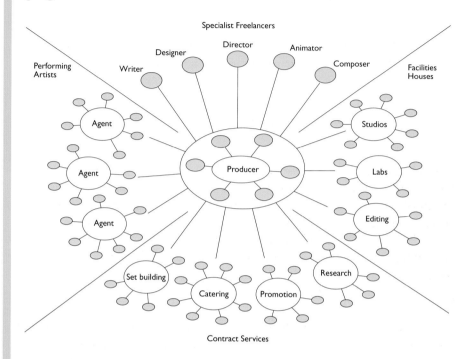

Figure 4.2 *The flexible TV production network*
Source: Barnatt and Starkey, 1994, p.258, Figure 4

Figure 4.2 is also a clear example of the 'dynamic' network mode of organization [...]. Networks configured around single projects dissolve upon project completion. In such configurations, the central core, 'the broker' role, is crucial. It is the producer/broker who sustains the network to 'operationalize its ideas', contracting out discrete key activities to its selected periphery nodes. [...] It should be noted that specialist freelancers are represented as sole agents in the TV network, whereas performing artists are depicted as sub-nodes working through agents. It is virtually impossible to gain employment as an actor, actress or musician other than through an agent. Within the other two periphery resource categories (facilities houses and contract services), each node is shown as the centre of its own network form, indicating that the use of freelance staff and outsourcing spans the breadth of TV production. Set builders, caterers, promotion and research companies are likely to hire in staff as required to handle current workload, and facilities houses may well turn to other facilities providers and/or freelance specialists on occasions in order to cope with production requirements which they are unable to handle internally.

Reference

BBC (British Broadcasting Corporation) (1992) *Extending Choice: The BBC's Role in the New Broadcasting Age*, London, BBC Publications.

Reading source

Barnatt and Starkey, 1994, pp.253–4, 257–8　■ ■ ■

Barnatt and Starkey contrast the new flexible arrangements with 'old, high-cost bureaucracies', which were 'rigid', unlike the 'dynamic' and (by implication) lower-cost flexible production. Their language represents an endorsement of the flexibly specialised networking structure over that which it is perceived to have replaced. This is a view that can be challenged on a number of grounds: the work of Georgina Born on the BBC, discussed in Chapter 2 in this book, points to a number of problems with the attempt to introduce such 'flexibility' into that organisation.

Certainly increasing flexibility was the perspective of UK Conservative governments of the 1980s and early 1990s. As mentioned above, these were governments committed to free-market economics – the view that unregulated markets were the best thing for business and society. Critics of the flexibility approach argued, in response, that a corporate structure that offered good earnings and permanent media employment was the best one in which to nurture talent, creativity, innovation and high-quality cultural production. Against this kind of criticism, Conservative governments insisted that it was the consumer who should decide what was produced, not the producers. In the particular instances of North American and UK film and television production, it is possible to say that much greater volumes of product are now being made without a pro rata increase in the numbers of workers employed, and that consumers have greater choice. The issues are not clear-cut, however. Many would say that increased consumer choice is more apparent than real and/or that much of what is available is of lower quality than before. Many experienced workers have left the industries, creating a shortage of suitable workers for some jobs. Moreover, it is not possible to claim that production costs are now generally lower. Rather, some areas of expenditure have been squeezed while others have been inflated. Marketing costs have soared in the film industry, for example, as a consequence of intensified product competition. Associated with higher marketing costs has been a sharp inflation in the sums paid to stars and celebrities. At the

Figure 4.3 John Birt, who, as Deputy Director General of the BBC from 1987 to 1992 and as Director General from 1992 to 2000, carried out controversial reforms, many of them aimed at increasing 'flexibility'
Source: BBC Photo Library

same time there has been a significant deflation in the earnings of other media workers, notably technical crews and new entrants, employed often at very low rates of pay.

What do Barnatt and Starkey have to say about the experience of media workers in this new flexible regime and how they cope? There are clues in their concept of 'network nodes'. This concept paints a picture of workers operating in specialist units, which, in their words, 'form the network nodes around a production core'. The ideas of networking and of freelance workers were introduced to discussions of flexibility as a result of numerous empirical investigations into how freelancers find work in these flexible employment regimes. Their self-directedness may not add up to the 'republic of small holders' applauded by Piore and Sabel, but certainly these workers are not inert economic resources waiting for management instructions. This suggests the importance of social relations to the success both of these media workers in finding paid work and also of the employers in finding competent workers. Those social relations can be explored more thoroughly within the broad parameters of a labour process approach, which we explore in the next section.

Before we move on, however, let us summarise the discussion of views of media work that see the media worker primarily as an economic resource (explored here via the concept of 'flexibility'). In many respects this perspective may seem highly appropriate. It correctly captures the actual developments and practices encouraged by UK and other governments in recent decades and introduced by many businesses in their search for higher labour productivity and lower production costs. Yet there is a danger that the approach misses the actual experience of media work and some of the negative consequences for society of a media system characterised by such flexible working arrangements.

One dimension that is under-explored by advocates of flexibility is the extent to which media workers are able to exert an influence over what they are making. Management approaches, which concentrate on economic results, see this issue as irrelevant. To investigate it, we need to look at alternative approaches, so let us move on.

3 Media workers as exploited under capitalism

The adoption in recent decades by governments and employers of free-market economic policies and practices has been hotly contested. Much of the argument and data mobilised in that contest has emanated from academics following the labour process approach (see the Introduction to this book). This approach tends to ask questions about workers' coping strategies, terms and conditions of employment, the functional and managerial division of labour and status hierarchies within workforces. Labour process analysis developed from Braverman's (1974) classic book predicting the degradation and deskilling of labour as an inevitable element in the development of capitalism. The fundamental assumption was that the owners of capital exercise power over those who must sell their labour power in order to survive. Building on these Marxist propositions, Braverman argued that profit-seeking corporations will strive continuously to increase their rate of exploitation of workers. To do this, he said, they will adopt strategies that enhance worker dependencies on employment, weaken labour collectivities, undermine any need for the skills of specialists and accelerate the rate of production. Corporate action to create large pools of casualised labour, refusals to negotiate with trade unions, the displacement of human labour by technology and speeded-up production regimes are predicated in the development of capitalism, according to Braverman.

Contemporary labour process writers tend to accept the view of capitalism as exploiting workers, but they disagree about the inevitability of degradation and deskilling, as we can explore in the context of the media. We will take UK broadcasting, film and newspapers as our case studies.

3.1 Broadcasting and film

Many observers of UK television since the late 1980s would say that the intensified exploitation of workers is exactly what has happened. They would point in evidence to Conservative government action to weaken the trade unions in general, and to diminish the earning power of broadcast workers in particular. The 1990 Broadcasting Act largely accepted the view of the 1986 Peacock Committee on broadcasting that:

> ...the broadcasting industry was wasteful of resources through over-manning [*sic*] and self-indulgent working practices. ... The costs for productions by the BBC and ITV [Independent Television – the main commercial terrestrial television company in the UK] have been compared with those for independent production which, it is suggested, are cheaper but just as good.'
>
> Home Office, 1986, para. 532

In 1988 to 1989, the commercial television franchise holders abandoned all nationally applying union–management agreements, and moved to plant-level consultations as distinct from negotiations. As mentioned earlier, from the late 1980s the numbers employed dropped dramatically. The consolidation of the 17 companies that operated ITV prior to 1990 into one company by 2002 has led to further reduction in staff positions, while advertising recessions have also led to a loss of work for freelancers. At my last count (Ursell, 2003) commercial terrestrial broadcasting in the UK employed about 5,000 as permanent staff and a further 5,000 as freelancers. This workforce of 10,000 people was responsible for the production of 50,000 annual programming hours. While rates of pay between staff and freelance positions have remained reasonably constant, earnings for freelancers have fallen in real terms on average by one-third. But the average obscures huge inequalities: those in constant demand do well and those who are not suffer. My own research (Ursell, 1998, 2000, 2003) among UK television workers (conducted across the years 1992 to 1996) provides illustrations of how some workers experienced these changes (see Box 4.1).

Box 4.1 Martin, a case study

Martin was a film editor with 12 years' length of service at the time I interviewed him. His television career came, in his words, to a 'grinding halt in 1992'. He commented, 'you think you're immune, that it won't happen to you, that you're quite good – I was working on *Brass Tacks* doing a programme on low pay and unemployment, never thinking it could happen to me.' Another man, Yorkshire based director/producer David, voluntarily became freelance in 1984 in the anticipation of greater creative freedom. In the first phase of his freelance status, his projects for Channel 4 had enjoyed budgets around £130,000 per single 40-minute documentary. The redundancy waves of the late 1980s left him competing in a much fuller labour market. Interviewed in 1993, he had then only 6 weeks work in prospect, but he was pitching for a satellite commission. This commission would involve him in making a 13-part series of 30-minute episodes for a total budget of £39,000. By 1996, he had bought himself a digital editing facility so as to eliminate the need to pay an online editor. His experience, he said, was 'awful'; if he had known what it would be like, he would have 'gone into teaching'. 'It's a lottery unless you're part of the London charmed circle ... if (your) name isn't known to the commissioner, your proposal won't get read.'

David's comments in Box 4.1 emphasise how both entry to and progression within the occupational communities of UK television production are contingent upon collegial ties, networking and individual reputation. We can explore these occupational communities in the context both of film and television (many audio-visual workers operate in the labour markets of both industries). Helen Blair's (2003) research illustrates how freelancers in the UK film industry find work, and it provides evidence to support the emphasis on negative worker experiences in the labour process approach. Blair says we need to recognise the importance of how workers organise themselves and each other in the labour markets upon which the employers draw. She points out that, unlike in the USA, in the UK there is no formal institutional mechanism whereby freelance film workers are allocated paid film production employment. Instead (and as a result), in the UK there have developed informal groupings of freelancers who regularly seek work together, groupings within which there are clear hierarchies of management as well as differentiated task responsibilities. Moreover, in the creation of these groupings, as in the securing of initial entry to the workforce and in the securing of paid working hours, the assistance of relatives, friends and friends-of-friends already in the industry is crucial. My own research confirms that these freelance relationships, informal groupings, hierarchies and networking exist equally in UK television labour markets.

The career of Chris, another of my television interviewees, reveals the importance of both contacts and curriculum vitae (CVs) (see Box 4.2). It also reveals, importantly, the extent to which some workers retain a great deal of control over their lives and their work activities, notwithstanding that they operate within an environment conditioned by profit-seeking employers. This helps to emphasise the importance of seeing workers as active agents, rather than as the passive economic units of the economic approach discussed in Section 2.

Box 4.2 Chris, a case study

Chris trained initially as a cameraman at Yorkshire Television, and was promoted through the grades to become (the higher status) lighting cameraman. He sought but was initially denied voluntary severance in the late 1980s as, in his terms, 'American management styles came in which were dreadful' and resulted in people 'being treated like idiots'. By 1991, he left television thinking it would not survive: 'I didn't want to be party to its demise'; 'I was going to return to painting, I was ready to survive on a low income'. But a friend, the managing director of a local independent, offered him the chance to work 'on a nice little quiz series' as lighting director with additional responsibilities to negotiate within a budget for staffing and facilities. In the same multi-functional role, he was subsequently approached by another independent ... 'He gave me a budget. I lit but also I supplied all the crew. ... I tend to use the same crew ... once you've got a good group around you, people you can rely on, keep together – it releases you to do your creative side.' This second project led to a third offer and, 'I realised my own potential, and a potential

to earn, so I decided to stay in the industry as a freelance'. But 'I'd
worked for a director in Central Nottingham on a kids' drama. She
wanted me for a BBC job. She showed me [another lighting
director's] CV, and he got the job. It made me realise how
important CVs are, so I reworked mine. I'd looked small time.
I was six months out of work in 1993, so I got out the Film Institute
book (which I'd joined) and I sent a CV to every company in it.
You've got to meet and eyeball people, you can't go cold on paper,
you must present yourself in the freelance market. After that, I got
lots of work.' 'My eldest son has now joined me ... he'd lighted
since age 14 at his school and he came with me on shoots and into
the studio. I gave him three months' trial and he showed a real
talent, firstly in being sociable, people liked him ... that's the
keystone of being able to work in this industry. Second is being
able to do the job well. He has his own company now, so do I, and
we contract each other. ... Between us we take on loads of work.'

The case of Chris also shows that, within the occupational communities
of television workers, a hierarchy of labour emerges that is reflective
of different degrees of occupational celebrity. But you will recall that
entry to these informal occupational communities has, to date, been
significantly conditioned by whether you have friends and relatives already
working in the industry: we can therefore describe these communities as
being 'partially closed', rather than open to all. An immediate implication
is that these informal arrangements can, unless consciously mitigated,
work to the disadvantage of unknown newcomers, those who are
culturally or politically different, and those whose domestic responsibilities
and/or limits of physical stamina restrict their availability for long and
anti-social hours of working. In other words, this contributes to the
negative picture of media work drawn by labour process theory, and to
the way in which social inequality is reproduced in media production,
extending the analysis beyond class inequality to gender, ethnicity and age.
The British Film Institute's (BFI) tracking surveys (BFI, 1997), which have
followed the employment experiences of film and television workers
across a number of years, have found that women, older people, and
people from minority ethnic backgrounds find it more difficult to find and
to keep employment. As one of their interviewees, Eileen, a film editor,
said 'There's no career structure these days – it's very damaging – there's
no element of security which allows people to make mistakes – there's no
mentoring in the freelance world.'
    Life for those on staff with a broadcaster is not much easier,
however. Diminished budgets (for all but the blockbusters aiming to sell
in international markets) and greater control over workers mimics those
'American management styles' which Chris found 'dreadful'. That he was

not alone in this judgement can be taken from the satirisation of an in-house appraisal scheme, as shown in Table 4.1. I found this doing the rounds in Yorkshire Television in 1994 but it was said to have originated in the BBC.

Table 4.1 An employee's view of performance appraisal

	A	B	C	D	E
Performance factors	Far exceeds job requirements	Exceeds job requirements	Meets job requirements	Needs to improve	Does not meet job requirements
Quality	Leaps tall buildings with single bound	Needs running start to leap tall buildings	Can only leap over buildings with no spires	Crashes into buildings when trying to jump	Cannot recognise buildings at all, let alone jump
Timeliness	Is faster than a speeding bullet	Is as fast as a speeding bullet	Not as fast as a speeding bullet	Would you believe a slow bullet?	Wounds self with bullet
Initiative	Is stronger than a locomotive	Is stronger than a bull elephant	Is stronger than a bull	Shoots the bull	Smells like a bull
Adaptability	Walks on water constantly	Walks on water in emergencies	Washes with water	Drinks water	Passes water in emergencies

In attempting to summarise and account for change in film and broadcasting employment, a labour process approach would point to the continuing (indeed, in places strengthening) control of employers over employees. The account would highlight the large pools of freelance workers and describe them as 'casualised labour', whose very presence undermines the security of those on permanent contracts and whose uncertain job prospects weakens their ability to organise into trade unions. The account would also point to the way in which these weaker, casualised workers organise informally so as to maintain some element of control over their lives. This is a picture in which the major employers have transferred many of the risks, costs and management tasks on to the workers themselves. But in the process, the employers have made themselves potentially vulnerable. They must now compete with other employers for workers on a project-by-project basis, which can be a problem if certain types of worker are in short supply and/or where a rival employer is offering better terms and conditions.

Additionally, research informed by a labour process perspective is likely to look at how the workers understand the employer's objectives in making the changes. We can suggest, for example, that the satirical version of the appraisal scheme shown in Table 4.1 is evidence of broadcast workers' critical distance from that particular management technique. Notwithstanding all the evidence of such critical distance, there is also much evidence of people's determination to continue working in the media as far as they can. These observations set a limit on the extent to which we can construe these workers as 'degraded' in the way that the Braverman thesis predicts. Certainly for many of them, their pay and conditions of employment have been degraded but Braverman seems to have meant something more than this, something to do with the denial of any creative input to the production process. It is the very possibility of making such an input that seems to enthuse these media workers, and explains their (often steely) determination to stay in the industry. We will return to these issues in Section 5.

3.2 The newspaper industry

While television and film industries have become characterised by a lot of outsourcing to subcontractors and a greater reliance on freelancers, the picture is different in the newspaper industry. Here, over the last three decades of the twentieth century, there were, rather, processes of centralised production, using smaller numbers of workers who were nonetheless more likely to be retained as permanent staff than employed on a freelance basis. These employment patterns are consistent with an industrial structure of concentration and conglomeration (Stokes and Reading, 1999; Curran and Seaton, 2003; see also Chapter 1). The pursuit by newspaper proprietors of higher labour productivity and improved corporate profitability in an increasingly competitive media environment has been behind these developments. Concentration refers to ownership of newspaper titles coming to reside in the hands of fewer and fewer proprietors. Conglomeration refers to those newspapers being increasingly subsumed within multimedia conglomerates (see Chapter 1). Diversification refers to the practice of these conglomerates of offering a very great range of alternative products to consumers. This is so as to create a very large total market by accumulating lots of small ones. My research into the Canadian and UK newspaper industries indicates striking similarities in their structural and employment arrangements, and both seem increasingly informed by US practices and values. Again, in my view, this helps to sustain a modified labour process view of the media industries.

Chain ownership of newspapers has perpetuated the survival of discrete provincial and national newspaper titles, but allows for substantial proportions of copy to be written and/or sub-edited centrally. New technologies have been implemented to facilitate such centralised production, while also displacing the craft print workers who previously composed the pages and ran the presses. In turn, the journalists have been required to become functionally flexible and multi-skilled in the sense of acquiring the technical competences and tasks of electronic page composition and inputting.

Simultaneous with the declining numbers of journalists in local offices, the demand for page-ready copy has become sufficiently large over the last twenty-five years that the major news agencies have been able to divide up their workforces into those who gather the raw data (the reporters) and those who take this data and write it up (the production journalists) for one or several different clients. The speed of production of the latter group is anchored to the house style of the client and to the number of pieces of copy to be produced in a given time. The processes of news production are thus here both standardised and routinised, while at the same time an occupational status division is created between those who gather news and those who process it. Bromley refers to the latter as 'technicians-with-words' (Bromley, 1997, p.346), which perhaps understates their need to know their subject. Arguably, it is a mixture of the idiosyncratic knowledge of journalists, corporate concerns to protect copyright and the significant scope for standardisation and routinisation in news production that explains why journalists, unlike workers in other sectors of the media, are less likely to be freelancers than are workers in the television and film industries.

3.3 Deskilling?

Let us now review what we have learned from Section 3. Whether using flexible employment practices or preferring centralised and permanent workforces, the labour process argument here is that the main media remain centrally controlled. Such radical transformation as has characterised the last 30 years has, so a labour process analyst would argue, driven corporate strategies to reduce labour costs and to create a more tractable workforce. She or he would cite as evidence the industrial disputes characterising the US film industry and the UK print industry of the 1980s, and the anti-union legislation of both countries over that same period. Some measure of the intensity of these 'politics of production' (Elger, 1991) is shown in Figure 4.4, a photograph from a bitter dispute that took place at the newly built premises of News International, the publisher of a number of leading UK national newspapers, in Wapping, East London, in 1986. Rupert Murdoch, the owner of News International, was seeking to break the British print unions and introduce electronic printing technologies at the cost of print workers' jobs. Print workers and their supporters fiercely resisted these moves and confrontations with police and with drivers entering the new plant were often violent.

Figure 4.4 *A clash between protestors and police during the 'Battle of Wapping'*
Source: BBC Photo Library

On the basis of this kind of evidence, a Braverman-type labour process analysis seems highly persuasive. But we still need to consider Braverman's contention that capitalism's pursuit of higher labour productivity inevitably leads to workers being deskilled. Let's look at the evidence in the media. It is true, for example, that video technology displaced the film format and contributed to the disappearance of huge, heavy cameras and very large camera and support crews. It also introduced a requirement that workers other than film-trained camera crew become competent in shooting and editing. But the film-trained camera crew has not disappeared entirely: the older film technology survives at the high-status end of television production, and with it survives the film-competent camera person/director and telecinist editor. More tellingly in relation to the Braverman thesis, other types of worker now possess competences in computer and/or video production. This includes some newspaper journalists, required by the employers increasingly to be able to turn out copy appropriate to a wide range of different media. These media workers cannot be represented as skilled specialists but they are skilled generalists. Is that the same as saying that they are less skilled? The same argument could be built around the application of computers to television production. The skills required to construct audio-visual material via a computer are certainly different from those involved in location and studio construction. But what precisely is it that we are construing as a skill, such that we can say one skill is higher or lower than another?

The skills required to put together a newspaper page on a computer are different from those required to put it together manually, using lots of individual letters composed on a flat stone. The apprenticeship for a compositor (the person who put the letters together on the stone) in the UK used to be seven years. The training for computer page composition is about one week. In your view, does this make computer page composition less 'skilled'? Think about what, in your opinion, being a skilled worker means, then read on. ■ ■ ■

The important point here is that 'skill' is not an absolute concept: it can be variously defined. Length of training might be one criterion, but so also might be (staying with our newspaper example) attractiveness to the reader. Speed of delivery might be another. Manual page composition takes a lot longer than computer page composition. In television, an outside broadcast crew of 30 needs more time to shoot and record than does a small video crew of three, which requires more time than a single video journalist. In other words, we would need to specify the criteria demarcating 'skill' before we could make any blunt assertion that media workers are nowadays less skilled than their predecessors.

With regard to degradation in the terms and conditions of employment, our task is easier and we have already addressed it in Section 3.1. The answer for many media workers is, simply, yes, as mentioned in Section 3.1, their terms and conditions *are* degraded. But are these workers then degraded in the sense of being made to feel low and miserable by their working lives? Is it the case that media workers have no say over what they produce and how they produce it? Is it the case that they have little control over the application and development of their abilities and talents? The evidence has revealed that, for many of them, self-direction is not only possible but essential both to themselves and to their employer. That evidence is difficult to reconcile with the original Braverman thesis.

We arrive here at a problem with the Braverman approach, one that has been taken to contaminate many Braverman-type analyses in terms of labour process and which has been characterised as 'the missing subject' (Manwaring and Wood, 1985). This criticism in essence says that the picture of capitalism generating exploitation ignores people's contribution to the making of their own and other people's life experiences. Some would say that Marxism, in its emphasis on the effects of capitalism, represents people as being made by the system, rather than the system being made by people. Yet it could be said that the case studies of film and television production *do* provide evidence, notwithstanding the economic powers of corporations, of the essential and voluntary contributions made by workers to the organisation and operations of these labour markets. Moreover, we can identify the way in which these same workers construct amongst themselves the status hierarchies of occupational stardom. Why are people volunteering for this kind of work, given all that we can say about the ratcheting up of production schedules, the increasingly constrained budgets, the insecurities of freelance work, and so on?

The clue lies in the following statements: from studio director Alice, 'You have to be very strong to work through the rubbish without it dragging you down. To be really good, money mustn't be the first thing, something artistic must drive you.' Or from Chris, the lighting director quoted in Box 4.2: 'A cameraman needs to be able to imagine the script, to work with the director, visualise and establish lighting [to support] speech rhythms, lulls in the narrative, particular scenes and so on. There's an excitement about taking an audience and entrancing them throughout the programme, taking them over in their emotions and experience. [...] You get a wonderful richness from a team of talented people who are well-tuned to each other.'

If, as a labour process account might argue, film and television production in the hands of profit-seeking corporations represents the exploitation of people's subjectivities, we need yet to consider what prompts people voluntarily to proffer their subjectivity for this treatment. The drive for personal artistry is suggested by Alice; an almost sensual relationship to audiences and to fellow workers is suggested by Chris. Something fundamental is going on here, and we must now consider two different attempts to theorise it: first, the worker who consciously strives to be a professional (Section 4), and second, the worker who is an individual in the process of making his or her self in an employment context (Section 5).

4   Media workers as professionals

The next approach sees media work in terms of its 'professional' nature. This is a highly contested term and there are no simple, universally accepted definitions. But integral to many discussions are assertions that 'professionals' play an important public service role, the conduct of which must fit with certain standards, for the benefit of clients and of society in general. 'Professional' work is often set in opposition to 'craft' work – though some journalists would argue that theirs is as much a craft as a profession (see Hallin, 2000, p.220). The theorisation of professionalism has passed through various stages, and the role of professionals in society has been differently judged. Emile Durkheim (1857–1917), a founding father of sociology, saw the professions as being good in the sense of constituting independent, expert and altruistic occupations, which functioned to bridge the gap between state and citizens and to ensure social integration (see Durkheim, 1957/1950). Some Marxists viewed these integrative functions much less positively than either Durkheim or other sociologists who were influenced by him – seeing the professions as reproducing the inequalities of capitalism. Although otherwise opposed, both the Marxists and the Durkheimians construed the professions as a distinct occupational category and recognised the following attributes: professional autonomy (see Chapter 2 for discussion of this important concept), the delineation of specific standards of conduct and competence and the operation of an authoritative peer association that could oversee and enforce these standards. With the late twentieth-century shift of Western economies to ever greater proportions of service and white-collar work, some writers anticipated the 'professionalisation of everyone' (Wilensky, 1964). The proof was to be established by measuring the extent to which any one occupation met the requirements of expertise, public or client service, knowledge acquisition, codes of conduct and accountability to peers (Greenwood, 1957). This approach was challenged by others, such as Hughes (1971) and Johnson (1972). They argued, first, that such a definition of professionalism was built too narrowly on the specific professions of law and medicine and, second, that professional status was not a 'given' but, rather, had to be negotiated with all other interested parties. (Negotiation here is a metaphor for the constant struggle over the meaning of the term, rather than explicit discussions around a table, as in the negotiations that take place over wage settlements.) In other words, they argued, we should recognise 'professionalism' as a claim for privileged occupational status and autonomy that is made by an occupational group and its members. We should also, they said, recognise that this claim has to be conceded by others if the status and autonomy is to be won.

This raises a number of interesting questions; for example, about the interests of the other parties who might dispute the claim and about the values and norms that are used to publicly judge and contest the occupation's role and performance. It also allows us to regard the claim 'I am a professional' to be a declaration of something like a property right, that is, 'this field of activity is mine and not yours'. In other words, it is an act of self and social identity formation. So the study of media workers as professionals allows us to see how, in media work as in all kinds of work, there are struggles over how to do things and why; and that in certain institutions and organisations at particular times, the notion of 'professionalism' is essential to this. We can explore these issues further in two readings, the first about newspaper journalists, the second about BBC staff.

4.1 Struggles over professionalism

One key area of debate about media work in recent years has concerned the recognition and respect accorded to journalists (Lloyd, 2004 provides one example). There are links here with some of the issues discussed in Section 2: that is, how have attempts to cut costs and increase productivity (whether through 'flexibility' or other means) affected the professional status of journalists? Let us take a look at the views of one newspaper journalist on this question.

Now read the following extract from Cleland Thom's work 'Spoon-fed and overspun', and answer the following questions:

- In what ways, in the judgement and experience of Cleland Thom, have changes in the numbers of journalists employed and in their conditions of work impacted on the qualities of local news reporting?
- On what grounds does Thom argue that this matters?

Reading 4.2

Cleland Thom, 'Spoon-fed and overspun'

The local paper where I was working as a sub was desperate for a reporter. Guess who drew the short straw? [...] I had left reporting behind 15 years earlier when I became a sub, then an editor, then a group editor, and then a journalism trainer. [...]

The experience was scary. [...] The world that our reporters are operating in now has changed beyond recognition. I found it almost impossible to get beyond the spin in the time allowed to produce a decent story.

Nowadays, everybody from the council to the police and even the local branch of the WI [the Women's Institute] has a spin doctor – or PR person, as we used to call them.

Over recent years, almost every redundant journalist has sold his soul and provided some media-management training for anybody and everybody who wants it – and now the chickens have come home to roost. Everyone you deal with knows how to handle journalists, how they operate, what they need, what they are likely to ask.

In some ways, this has great benefits for hard-pressed local journalists. Having a PR-trained public means you get stories that are gift-wrapped, served on a plate. [...]

For the busy reporter, struggling to produce more copy to tighter deadlines with a smaller staff, it's a godsend. Local reporting was never quicker. No more chasing people or waiting for contacts to phone you back. You get everything spoon-fed to you.

So what could be wrong with that?

As I said earlier, the experience was scary, because it suddenly dawned on me that the stories I was conveniently being given were simply the ones that the authorities wanted me to write. And there often wasn't time to dig any deeper.

[...] local papers can easily become nothing more than a mouthpiece of local organisations such as the council and the police. We can end up singing their song and telling their news the way they want us to. This has serious implications for local democracy and the local paper's role as a watchdog and a public conscience. [...]

Colleges and training establishments need to drum it into trainees far more than they do now that they must get behind spin doctors, the briefings and the PR men [*sic*]. They must resist being spoon-fed the stories that authorities want you to have. They must upset apple carts and ask awkward questions.

Reading source

Thom, 2002, p.17 ▪ ▪ ▪

Thom, in commenting on a number of changes in newspaper journalism, shows great concern for the attributes of the newspaper as a product and the ability of journalists to maintain high standards. It is apparent that he sees the changes as constituting a threat to democracy; that is, he is making direct links between conditions of employment of media professionals, the character of the media product and the consequences for the wider society. We see here that Thom is revealing himself as a member of an occupational group that lays claim to a professionalism defined in terms of journalists being a public 'watchdog'. For a journalist in a democracy, professionalism is defined very much in terms of delivering factually based, comprehensive, fairly reported and speedy news about important events and people to the public. That there are so many occasions when particular journalists or papers are berated for poor standards shows how alive and assertive is this vision of what the 'good' professional journalist should be doing.

Aspiring to and being treated as a professional is one major way in which individuals can claim an entitlement to practise a high degree of autonomy in their employment: they are the experts and they know best. But it is not as simple as that. Thom's piece shows not only the continuing authority of employers but also the significance of changed practices among the other organisations upon which journalists rely as sources. We can discover further complications from Reading 4.3 below. This is taken from Tom Burns's book on the BBC in the 1960s and 1970s. It is helpful to note that his research was prompted by government action to impose management consultants on the Corporation with a remit to improve efficiency and reduce costs.

Read the following extract from Tom Burns's book *The BBC: Public Institution, Private World* and answer these questions:

- According to Burns, how did the term 'professional' come to be so widely used in the BBC of the 1960s and 1970s?
- What is his attitude towards the term?

Reading 4.3

Tom Burns, 'A private world'

The word 'professional' had, by 1963, an extraordinarily wide currency throughout the BBC. There were times when it seemed that the word was being credited among programme staff with an almost talismanic quality, representing some absolute principle by which to judge people and achievement. Ten years later the word seemed to occur ... more frequently, to have acquired a wider and more potent range of meanings and connotations, and to be used throughout all reaches of the Corporation. Among senior management in charge of television and radio it had assumed the character of some ultimate rationale. [...]

The sheer frequency of its occurrence, the variety of contexts in which it was brought into play, and the very heavy load of judgement and appraisal it was intended to carry all suggest that members of the Corporation used the word 'professional' as a kind of semantic credit card with which they could shop around a wide range of desirable ascriptions and attributes. By contrast, one hardly ever encounters this evaluative use of the word among people in those occupations which are regarded as professions in the classic, paradigmatic, sense – law and medicine. [...] Where the word 'professional' frequently is used is in those occupations which find a continuing need to discriminate between the attitudes, the *modus operandi*, the competence, experience, training qualifications and the quality of result which, it is claimed, can be expected from those whom one recognises as 'professionals' as against 'laymen' [*sic*] or 'amateurs'. [...]

In the context of the BBC, 'professionalism' also involved 'dedication', 'commitment'. [...]

The increasing salience of such preoccupations is a further, and definitive, mark of the transition of broadcasting from an occupation dominated by the ethos of public service, in which the central concern is with quality in terms of the public good, and of public betterment, to one dominated by the ethos of professionalism, in which the central concern is with quality of performance in terms of standards of appraisal by fellow professionals; in brief, a shift from treating broadcasting as a means to treating broadcasting as an end.

Professionalism as a moral order

[...] The spread of the currency of the term 'professional' throughout all the upper reaches of the Corporation and the increased frequency of its use seem to me to mark three separate, but related, trends. The first [... relates] to the technical division of labour. The second trend is [...] in the form of associations (nowadays frequently 'white-collar unions') as strategic instruments for gaining autonomy, mostly relating to power to control admission to an occupation and the reservation to members of the association of certain kinds of work, but also so as to resist 'outside' control, whether it be from management, governmental agencies, or the client public. [...] Lastly, and most importantly, the word 'professional' is very frequently used in contexts which imply the invocation of some kind of moral order in which professional judgements, decisions, and actions are grounded. The moral order endows them with a legitimacy and authority which are regarded as distinguishable from, and at times superior to, contractual obligations, loyalty to the organisation, or compliance with public or other 'outside' demands or claims. [...]

[...] As soon as one particular specialism establishes its claim to professional standing, other people with jobs requiring a unique set of qualifications either obtained by education and training or derived from special qualities of sensibility, flair, intelligence, or verbal and social skills which have been refined, developed, and tested by experience are moved to make the same claim. And with the same professionalist notion of unique qualification for a particular kind of work goes the 'mandate to define what is proper conduct of others towards matters concerning their work'. This involves the disqualification of outsiders, which includes managers, not only from doing that kind of job themselves, but, effectively, from competence to evaluate performance. [...]

So, below the surface meaning of the expertness one expects from a full-time worker, or practitioner, or a 'pro', as against an amateur [...] there are quite explicit connotations of entitlement, of the licence and the mandate conferred on acknowledged members of a body of professionals; of criteria of professional competence which are claimed to be independent of any judgements by laymen, or clients, or the public at large; and, thirdly, a code of professional conduct which serves as a *quid pro quo* for that independence.

Reading source
Burns, 1977, pp.122–6, 131–2 ■ ■ ■

Burns shows how the term 'professional' helps certain media workers to deal with the conflicts of the workplace (cf. Elliott, 1977, p.150). He takes a cool, dispassionate view of the term, showing how it spread through the BBC, rather than taking it at face value as a positive term.

His account allows us to reflect on the *relational* and *negotiated* status of media professionalism. It is relational in the sense of identifying a specific collectivity and delineating who is or is not a member, and it is both relational and negotiated in the sense of being constrained by essential relationships with other authoritative parties, such as the government and the BBC as employers. That claims to professional status became the 'semantic credit card' of this period was, according to Burns, substantially an effort to ward off the 'inappropriate' judgements and decision recommendations of the management consultants. (As Burns was writing about events in the 1960s and 1970s, this suggests that the 'flexibility' reforms discussed in Section 2 and in Born's 2004 account – see also Chapter 2 in this book – are not unprecedented.) Government action, however, to impose certain forms of management on the BBC was and remains constrained by political considerations of the power of the media in swaying electoral opinion. Similarly, BBC management faces the perpetual challenge of wresting compliance from specialist occupations and individuals whose performance is both crucial to the Corporation but simultaneously requires the exercise of considerable autonomy. In short, the occupational autonomy of media professionals is significant but it has to be negotiated and renegotiated with others – it is a relative autonomy (cf. Chapter 2). The terms of its negotiation will be the terms specified by the occupational group as distinguishing and legitimating its claim to professional status. Thus it could be argued that, in the phenomenon of media professionalism, we have an illustration of the dispersed and discursively constructed power that many theorists claim properly describes power in Western societies in recent decades. This links us to the next section, but first, let us briefly summarise what we have learned from this section.

We have seen that, while claims both to belong to a 'profession' and for 'professionalism' are common and widespread in media work, such claims have been analysed by some (for example, Burns) with scepticism. It is perhaps too cynical to say that claims to professionalism are entirely self-serving, but some would stress this aspect. Others, while recognising that professionalism is a relational and negotiated matter, would emphasise the potentially positive social results – for example, in encouraging journalists to resist 'commercialisation' (for example, Hallin, 2000). The analysis of professionalism is another important approach to media work and one that moves beyond the economic concerns of the first two approaches towards a more sociological concern with how people construct their identities at work, and towards consideration of the social impact of media work. The next approach is also sociologically rather than economically oriented.

Try to apply a labour process approach to Cleland Thom's experiences as a journalist. Do you think that Thom's account of the changes in a newspaper journalist's job supports Braverman's ideas that the development of capitalism inevitably leads to a deskilled workforce? See the end of this chapter for one possible answer. ■ ■ ■

5 Media workers, identity and discourse

Recent years have seen a long-term rise in non-manual, service sector employment in advanced industrial societies (Routh, 1980; Castells, 1996). The media industries are an important part of this increase. While such increases are driven by a variety of factors, including the increasing importance of leisure expenditure in such societies, it still remains intriguing that so many people *want* to work in the media industries. For some, the work of Michel Foucault has provided some useful insights into understanding such desire.

5.1 Foucault, Rose and 'self-actualisation'

In Foucault's writings we find the assertion that contemporary advanced society is characterised by a 'new technology of the self'. This can be defined as a system for allowing the construction of personal identities within a society. The concept of 'technology of the self' is a difficult one and involves the notion of 'subjectification', by which Foucault meant two things. The first is the historical process by which people in advanced societies have come to identify the 'self' (that is, the individual subject being) as an object, something that it is appropriate to lay open to critical investigation and considered management and manipulation (see Foucault, 1970). Foucault identified the emergence of the social sciences, mental institutions and psychiatry as evidence of this. The second meaning of subjectification is embedded in Foucault's notion of discourse (knowledge, beliefs, codes, conventions and practices). For Foucault, each one of us absorbs into the making of our individual self the main discourses of the social environment within which we exist. Moreover, we express and realise our individual self through this discourse and thus construct its production and reproduction. In this sense, argued Foucault, power is *dispersed* throughout all levels and spheres of the social. It is analytically inadequate, he said, to associate power narrowly with one source of dominance, such as capitalists or the state. Thus, the particular 'technology of the self' of the present discursive epoch constructs the self (that is, the subject individual) as an object to be acted upon, 'made' and 'remade', in a considered fashion by the individual at least as much as by authoritative social institutions.

Foucault's work is not without its critics, who typically challenge him on his version of history and on his dismal view of humanity (for example, Merquior, 1991). However, we shall investigate the implications of Foucault's thesis for media workers by turning to the work of the British sociologist Nikolas Rose. Rose is interested in the changing mechanisms of governability, that is, in what makes people behave themselves. He traces mutations in conceptions of subjectivity and technologies of the self from the mid nineteenth century to the present. Today, Rose says, the issue is not the governability of society but the governability of the passions of self-identifying individuals and collectivities. Increasingly, he says, 'individuals and pluralities are shaped not by the citizen-forming devices of church, school and public broadcasting but by commercial consumption regimes and the politics of lifestyle. [...] [T]he individual is identified by allegiance with one of a plurality of cultural communities' (Rose, 1999, pp.86–7). This is 'civilization through identification' (p.87), regulation through desire, consumption and the market.

Moreover, it links to conceptions of individual choice and autonomy. Thus 'freedom is redefined: it is no longer freedom from want [...] it is the capacity for self-realisation which can be obtained only through individual activity' (p.145). Moreover, 'leading a life in the contemporary world is a matter of the fabrication of identities within personal projects of self-actualisation in a whole variety of practices and sites' (pp.190–1). One of these 'sites' is work: 'The productive subject is to be governed ... as an individual striving for meaning in work, seeking identity in work, whose subjective desires for self-actualisation are to be harnessed to the firm's aspirations for productivity, efficiency and the like' (p.244).

Rose's last observation here re-engages the debate about subjectivity with debates about flexibility, labour process and professionalism. It enables us to reflect further on our objects of study, namely media workers, and to seek particular instances in which they might be described as realising and reproducing a discourse that simultaneously facilitates, relies upon and extracts public functions and/or commercial profits from their self-actualisation. Let us apply such ideas now to the contemporary media labour market in the UK.

5.2 The lure of media work

Many people want to work within the media industries. There is a permanent over-supply of labour in this field with fewer jobs than people chasing them. This phenomenon is curious for a number of reasons.

First, gaining employment as a new entrant is expensive in that typically it requires the student to assume responsibility for the time and financial costs of becoming suitably trained and knowledgeable. Second, for the audio-visual media, entry can also be very difficult: as already discussed, it helps greatly if you have friends or relatives in the business already. Third, new entrants are poorly paid in the main media of film, broadcasting and newspapers. There is no immediate financial return on the personal investment made by the student in securing appropriate qualifications. What then helps explain the manifest interest of so many of the younger generations in working in the media?

Recall that at the end of Section 3 we quoted Alice talking about the need for artistic drive to help her through the 'rubbish' of media employment. Remember also Chris's revelation of the pleasure he was able to take in moving the emotions of audiences, and from working within a 'well-tuned' group of competent and committed others. Recall too that the structuring of professional status, on analysis, reveals the experiencing and assertion of one's specialism as both a property right and a common identity with similar specialists. In short, pleasure, self-expression, self-enterprise and self-actualisation in public and group settings seem to be at the heart of the explanations of why people want to work in the media. This links up with the Foucault/Rose perspective that we nowadays actively 'make' ourselves, but we do so in terms of discourses that are profoundly social.

Ours is a culture informed by the values and perspectives of consumerism, liberalism and capitalism. It is a culture in which the values and practices of self-expression, self-enterprise and self-actualisation are widely endorsed and exhorted. One of the principal social institutions involved in such endorsement and exhortation is the media. Individual identity formation can be said to be strongly influenced by the media-constructed and conveyed branding and logos of consumer products: 'I'm a streetwise person because I wear Nike', 'I'm affluent, young and fun-loving; therefore I meet my friends in Starbucks', and so on. Support for a football team or player can, with media help, be expressed at an individual and group level in clothing, activities, hairstyles, coffee mugs, magazines, and so on. The media have, as it were, wrapped themselves around the identity formation processes of individuals in ways that not only sell products but also influence how people characterise and associate with each other and how, importantly, they experience pleasure.

Much of the recent growth in media industries reflects growth in audience demand for media (re)presentations of lifestyle material, for example, fashion, holidays, driving, gardening, travel. In responding to those demands, the media become involved in (re)producing the aspirations and dreams of the audiences and, thereby, the public articulation and expression of their pleasures. The media are, as it were, both the weavers and the sellers of dreams.

Additionally, the media are public arenas in which is displayed and enacted much of the stuff of contemporary political life. They are the primary arena in which citizens can intellectually and emotionally engage with the major events and personnel of their social world. If the pleasure of self-actualisation is feeling yourself to be someone who is socially involved in ways that make a difference, whom other people regard with affection, respect, admiration and/or envy, and if you experience the media on a daily basis as both arenas of significant public activity and as weavers and sellers of dreams, then why not seek to pursue self-actualisation by working in the media? In that way, not only are your personal identity and status associated with these important institutions, but you become directly involved in the techniques and performances of public communication and dream-weaving. The media provide places to work in ways that may allow the expression of your ideas, preferences, artistry. Simultaneously, this is a place to play, have fun, experiment, rub up against the rich and famous, have privileged access to stories and gossip, be where the action is. You might become, according to this analysis, a more interesting person in your own eyes and those of others, because you work in the media. If you have to pay to get the training that facilitates your entry to the media, so be it. Media employment is a symbolic property and a site for potential self-actualisation that you might willingly purchase. These processes arguably confirm Foucault's assertions about discourse, subjectification and dispersed power, at least as translated by Nikolas Rose, with this stress on 'the fabrication of identities within personal projects of self-actualisation in a whole variety of practices and sites' (Rose, 1999, p.190–1) and on the 'individual striving for meaning in work, seeking identity in work' (p.244).

How does this type of argument relate to the potential for self-direction and autonomy of media workers in their employment context?

Certainly it offers a persuasive explanation of the attractiveness of media employment to many, and of people's capacity to create informal occupational communities that cultivate their own hierarchies and status discriminations. But it also seems to be arguing that the 'self-directedness' of media workers is something of an illusion, in that the 'self' can never be anything other than a socially, discursively, constructed phenomenon. We cannot shape our own selves, rather they are shaped by the discourses circulating in society. The heavy weight of social determinism in this vision questions the individualist ethos of liberal consumer society.

This is where criticism of the conception of power as employed by Foucault comes in. Instead of adopting the traditional perspective, which sees power as emanating from elites who enjoy superior command over economic and political resources, Foucault argues that it is dispersed across all relationships (see, for example, Foucault, 1980; 1982). Each one of us locks each other into relationships of power, hierarchy and status differentiation. We do this through processes of identity formation and self-direction. We – not 'they' – are the entrepreneurs. We – not 'they' – constantly strive at self- and other management. We call this 'freedom'. Power does not just work over subjects, it works through them too.

This view of power is problematic on two counts. One, it detracts attention from the elites whose economic and political decision making continues demonstrably to shape the life experiences and possibilities of the many. Two, it makes us all equally responsible for everything. Power is everywhere, therefore power is nowhere. Critics of Foucault (for example, Merquior, 1991) would argue that this is not only untenable, it is also politically unhelpful. Consider, for example, the situation of our media freelancers. Some will have volunteered for this status, this identity, but even more have had it forced upon them. Film and broadcast employers shed responsibility for the welfare and management of many of their workers, obliging those people to assume such responsibilities. The freelancers became self-managing and self-entrepreneurial in response to actions taken by employers over which they have had no effective say. In becoming self-managing and self-entrepreneurial, the freelancers are helping to make the film and broadcasting systems work. But how useful is it to adopt Foucault's perspective on this situation and say that power is diffused and therefore everyone is equally responsible? We cannot resolve these issues here, but they represent fundamental problems in interpreting contemporary media work.

6 Conclusion

Through the refracting lenses of different theoretical perspectives, we have considered the implications of changes in work and employment in film, broadcasting and the press. In the process, we have learned much that is practical. We have also seen that the different theoretical perspectives are very different normatively – that is, in terms of how they evaluate the employment relationship and occupations in the media context. They often highlight different aspects of the same phenomena or offer alternative interpretations of commonly perceived aspects of media work.

Thus, flexibility writers have described for us forms of labour deployment and employment in which responsibilities and risks have been devolved down on to the shoulders of workers and small specialised units (Section 2). This devolution has been proposed as a rational organisational response to the heightened uncertainties and greater risks of economies in recent decades. The concept of flexibility has analytically been applied to employees as an abstract category, and flexibility writers have paid scant attention to the experience of these people, and their contribution to labour markets and to production. There is little consideration of the potential of workers for self-directedness; rather, the focus is on employer techniques in managing the economic resource of labour so as to achieve higher productivity.

Activity 4.3

Try to apply the labour process and identity/discourse approaches discussed in this chapter to Chris's statements at the end of Section 3.3. See the end of this chapter for one possible answer. ▪ ▪ ▪

By applying the critical perspectives of labour process analyses (Section 3), we were able to reveal important aspects of that worker experience. Asserting the importance of recognising the continued control and exploitative character of large corporations, labour process analysts repudiate positive claims for flexible employment and production arrangements, instead arguing that intensification of work, increased insecurity of employment and lowered earning capacities are significant and negative features of flexibility. At the same time, applied to the media, this analytical approach has also highlighted the fundamental contribution that informal worker networking makes to production, to labour market processes and to the hierarchical ordering of the division of labour.

However, in the media context, Braverman's idea of the workforce as degraded and deskilled labour was revealed as problematic. The terms and conditions of employment for many media workers have clearly been degraded over recent decades, but this cannot automatically be taken to imply that they take less satisfaction from their work – a fact on which the employers rely. Similarly, the employers' new arrangements frequently translate into a demand for more and higher skills rather than fewer and lower. The labour process approach has revealed the constitutive role that workers, individually and collectively, play in the production process, but the Braverman thesis may not be able to deal with this role adequately.

In an attempt to redress this weakness, we moved on to consider two further bodies of theory, namely the analysis of media work as 'professionalism' and the Foucauldian approach to identity, discourse and power (Sections 4 and 5 respectively). Professionalism in the media we saw as an occupational status to be enjoyed only where the occupation could convince others of the social importance of its performance and of the high standards of that performance. We viewed it, in other words, as an example of a socially, discursively constructed identity. We also looked at two instances in which professional media practitioners felt their capacity for self-directed work activity to be threatened by employer action in pursuit of greater organisational efficiency. Professional identity in these instances became simultaneously the yardstick by which employment change was to be measured, and the weapon employed in the resistance of such change.

Recognising the significance of 'professionalism' to the construction of occupational identity in the media, we moved on to Foucault's concepts of subjectification and discourse. This approach enabled us to identify the significance of media employment as an arena of potential self-actualisation, to which people are attracted because the media are primary instruments in (re)producing discourses of self-actualisation, self-enterprise and identity formation, all aspects being profoundly social in their delineation and negotiation.

All four perspectives have something to say about the extent to which media workers are subject to the superior economic powers of their employers. In the first, the media worker is an economic resource to be deployed at the employer's discretion. Little or no attention is given to the potential of the worker to make a unique and self-directed contribution to (or indeed, against) the production process. Power here resides with the employer and is exercised over workers.

In the second perspective, the media worker is not only an economic resource for the employer but is also an individual capable of acting, alone or collectively, in ways independent of the employer. These ways may be in 'resistance' to the employer, or they may substitute for the employer in the recruitment and management of workers (and thereby, in the absorption of production responsibilities and costs). Workers remain subject to the superior economic powers of the employers, but their contribution to the labour process is not narrowly limited by that. Indeed, without the voluntary and informal contributions of media workers, the employers would be disadvantaged and production would suffer.

In the third perspective, the workers themselves collectively forge and promote their occupational identity as professionals. This is contested terrain in that the identity must be accepted beyond the members of the occupational community. But, where it is so accepted, it can be mobilised in an effort to defend occupational norms and working practices against any perceived threat from employers or, as in the case of the BBC, interventions from government. The autonomy of the media professional is, though, never absolute. Rather, it is perpetually relative to the powers of the employer and/or government, and will be likely to require recurrent renegotiation with those more powerful institutions. In those renegotiations, appeals may well be made to the wider public for support of one or other position. This is because public opinion is involved in giving legitimation to the professional status claims of the occupational community. So the identity of 'media professional' can be seen as discursively constructed and sustained.

This reflection leads on to our fourth perspective, on the importance of identity formation in contemporary society and the considered cultivation of 'self'. But in this perspective the economic and political powers of employers and government disappear from view. Rather, power is diffused and present in all relationships. This is because, according to this perspective, the 'self' is nowadays discursively constituted to accept as natural the tasks of self-entrepreneurship and self-management. Through processes of identity formation, the 'self' discriminates itself as unique from all others and performs in terms of the discrimination.

By way of final summary, Table 4.2 describes each approach in terms of i) its principal assumptions, ii) its empirical focus, iii) what it draws our attention to, and iv) what conclusions it comes to about the exercise of power between employers and workers in the media.

Table 4.2 Four approaches to media employment: a summary of main points

	Approach			
	Economic resource	Exploited worker	Professional	Constructed in discourse
Principal assumptions	Workers exist as a source of labour power	Owners of capital use labour power to make profits; workers can resist; degradation of skill	Distinct occupations exist, with social or client goals	Occupational identity is constructed in discourse
Empirical focus	The firm	Labour force, labour market	Occupations in society	Symbols, codes and meanings
Attention drawn to	Employer strategies for business structure and employment; trends and changes in economic organisation	Worker response to employer-led strategies and tactics; trends in economic organisation; trends in industrial relations; trends in patterns of work and employment	Institutional articulation of claims to expert or moral superiority; claims to ownership of the job; forms of collective organisation	Identity construction and experimentation in self-actualisation; the production and reproduction of systems of belief and practice in everyday life
Concept of Power	Power is vested in rights of economic ownership	Employers have power but workers resist and qualify it	Power is not power; this is rather the exercise of authority	Power is not power; everyone has some: that is, it is dispersed. We are all responsible for it

Answers to activities

Activity answer 4.2

Although Thom describes a work environment that involves 'tighter deadlines' and 'smaller staff', which would seem to indicate a worsening of conditions at work, he also argues for a keen sense of professional responsibility to fight against 'gift-wrapped' stories. The potential for deskilling is there (the journalist could simply accept the PR releases instead of completing their own investigations). However, Thom indicates his own determination to resist this process of deskilling. This 'professionalism' is best described by the approach discussed in Section 4. ▪▪▪

Activity answer 4.3

Chris's comment, in Section 3.3, is consistent with the view that work – and especially perhaps media work – is an important way in which people attempt to 'realise' themselves in modern societies. He speaks of the excitement of engaging with the audience and the 'wonderful richness' of working well with others. Whereas labour process theory might believe that Chris is ripe for exploitation, Foucauldians would be interested in the way in which such statements reflect prevailing discourses in modern societies about how people conduct themselves at work, and see work as central to their personal identities. ▪▪▪

Further reading

Blyton, P. and Morris, J. (eds) (1991) *A Flexible Future? Prospects for Work and Organisation*, Berlin, New York, de Gruyter. This is a series of essays that explore conceptually and/or investigate empirically a range of instances and developments in work and employment practices, especially 'flexible employment techniques'.

Golding, P. and Elliott, P. (1979) *Making the News*, London/New York, Longman.

Schlesinger, P. (1992/1978) *Putting Reality Together*, London, Routledge. These two classic studies provide important insights into how broadcast journalists have understood the social and civic role ascribed to them and how these understandings help to shape the news.

Gordon, C. (ed.) (1980) *Michel Foucault: Power/Knowledge*, New York/London, Harvester Wheatsheaf. This book explores Foucault's ideas and provides insight into their historical location in the intellectual revolutions of the post-Second World War period.

Gray, L.S. and Seeber, R.L. (eds) (1996) *Under the Stars: Essays on Labor Relations in Arts and Entertainment*, Ithaca, NY, ILR Press, Cornell University. This set of essays covers four sectors (live performing arts, recordings, motion pictures and broadcasting) in the USA and throws valuable light on some of the major issues of today with regard to employment and work in the media.

Thompson, P. and Warhurst, C. (eds) (1998) *Workplaces of the Future*, London, Routledge. This set of essays offers a range of critical perspectives on late twentieth-century work and employment change and introduces consideration of 'subjectivity' to the analysis.

References

Aksoy, A. and Robins, K. (1992) 'Hollywood for the 21st century: global competition for critical mass in image markets', *Cambridge Journal of Economics*, vol.16, pp.1–22.

Atkinson, J. (1984) 'Manpower strategies for flexible organisations,' *Personnel Management*, August, pp.28–31.

Barnatt, C. and Starkey, K. (1994) 'The emergence of flexible networks in the UK television industry', *British Journal of Management*, vol.5, pp.251–60.

BBC (British Broadcasting Corporation) (1992) *Extending Choice: The BBC's Role in the New Broadcasting Age*, London, BBC Publications.

BFI (British Film Institute) (1997) *Television Industry Tracking Studies: 2nd Interim Report*, London, BFI.

Blair, H. (2003) 'Winning and losing in flexible labour markets: the formation and operation of interdependence in the UK film industry', *Sociology*, vol.37, no.4, pp.677–94.

Born, G. (2004) *Uncertain Vision: Birt, Dyke and the Reinvention of the BBC*, London, Secker and Warburg.

Braverman, H. (1974) *Labor and Monopoly Capital*, New York, Monthly Review Press.

Bromley, M. (1997) 'The end of journalism' in Bromley, M. and O'Malley, T. (eds) *A Journalism Reader*, London, Routledge.

Burns, T. (1977) *The BBC: Public Institution, Private World*, London, Macmillan.

Castells, M. (1996) *The Rise of the Network Society*, Oxford, Blackwell.

Christopherson, S. and Storper, M. (1989) 'The effects of flexible specialisation on industrial politics and the labor market: the motion picture industry', *Industrial and Labor Relations Review*, vol.42, no.3, pp.331–47.

Curran, J. and Seaton, J. (2003) *Power without Responsibility: The Press and Broadcasting in Britain* (6th edn), London, Routledge.

Durkheim, E. (1957/1950) *Professional Ethics and Civic Morals* (trans. and ed. C. Brookfield), London, Routledge and Kegan Paul.

Elger, T. (1991) 'Task flexibility and the intensification of labour in UK manufacturing in the 80s' in Pollert, A. (ed.) *Farewell to Flexibility?*, Oxford, Blackwell.

Elliott, P. (1977) 'Media organisations and occupations: an overview' in Curran, J., Gurevtich, M. and Woollacott, J. (eds) *Mass Communication and Society*, London, Edward Arnold.

Foucault, M. (1970) *The Order of Things: An Archaeology of the Social Sciences*, London, Tavistock.

Foucault, M. (1980) *Power/Knowledge: Selected Interviews and Other Writings, 1972–1977* (trans. and ed. C. Gordon), Brighton, Harvester Press.

Foucault, M. (1982) 'The subject and power' in Dreyfuss, L. and Rabinow, P. (eds) *Michael Foucault*, Brighton, Harvester Press.

Greenwood, E. (1957) 'Attributes of a profession', *Social Work 2*, no.3, pp.45–55.

Hallin, D.C. (2000) 'Commercialism and professionalism in the American news media' in Curran, J. and Gurevitch, M. (eds) *Mass Media and Society* (3rd edn), London, Arnold.

Home Office (1986) *Report into the Financing of the BBC*, Cmnd 9824, London, HMSO (Peacock Committee).

Hughes, E.C. (1971) *The Sociological Eye*, New York, Aldine Atherton.

Johnson, T. (1972) *Professions and Power*, London, Macmillan.

Lloyd, J. (2004) *What the Media Are Doing to Our Politics*, London, Constable.

Manwaring, T. and Wood, S. (1985) 'The ghost in the labour process' in Knights, D., Willmott, H. and Collins, D. (eds) *Job Redesign: Critical Perspectives on the Labour Process*, Aldershot, Gower.

Merquior, J.G. (1991) *Foucault* (2nd edn), London, Fontana.

Piore, M. and Sabel, C. (1984) *The Second Industrial Divide: Possibilities for Prosperity*, New York, Basic Books.

Rose, N. (1999) *Powers of Freedom: Reframing Political Thought*, Cambridge, Cambridge University Press.

Routh, G. (1980) *Occupations and Pay in Great Britain, 1906–1979*, London, Macmillan.

Skillset (1996) *Labour Force Surveys: Key Findings and Comments, Briefing for RTS*, Skillset conference, London, Skillset.

Stokes, J. and Reading, A. (eds) (1999) *The Media in Britain: Current Debates and Developments*, London, Macmillan

Thom, C. (2002) 'Spoon-fed and overspun', *UK Press Gazette*, 5 July, p.17.

Ursell, G. (1998) 'Labour flexibility in the UK commercial television sector', *Media, Culture and Society*, vol.20, no.1, pp.129–54.

Ursell, G. (2000) 'Television production: issues of exploitation, commodification and subjectivity in UK television labour markets', *Media, Culture and Society*, vol.22, pp.805–25.

Ursell, G. (2001) 'Dumbing down or shaping up: new technology, new media, new journalism?' in *Journalism: Theory, Practice and Criticism*, vol.2, no.2, pp.175–96.

Ursell, G. (2003) 'Creating value and valuing creation in contemporary UK television: or "dumbing down" the workforce', *Journalism Studies*, vol.1, no.1, pp.31–46.

Wilensky, H. (1964) 'The professionalisation of everyone?', *American Journal of Sociology*, vol.70, pp.137–48.

Production and media analysis

David Hesmondhalgh

In the Introduction I explained that the three main themes running through the volume (and through the *Understanding Media* series as a whole) are power; knowledge, values and beliefs; and change and continuity, and I outlined some key questions asked by the book. In this Conclusion, I want to summarise briefly what the chapters have contributed to our understanding of these fundamental themes of media analysis.

Power

Do the media as a whole ultimately serve the interests of the wealthy and powerful? John Downey in Chapter 1 reported on the concerns of the political economy approach to media and culture, about the concentration of producer power in the hands of big business, and about links between media businesses and the machinery of the state (the example of Silvio Berlusconi in Italy was a striking example of such links). But Downey also raised the complicating factor that the drive for profit leads to complex dynamics which do not directly support the interests of one particular group. It is possible to read this as meaning that power is not just concentrated around a set of converging interests, but that it is also relatively dispersed when it comes to media production. My look at media organisations in Chapter 2 homed in further on this issue. The chapter contrasted a view of media production organisations as propagandists (developed by Herman and Chomsky) with three more complicated notions of power in critical media studies: an emphasis on the gaining of consent and of contestation in Gramscian and Bourdieuian perspectives on crime reporting; a treatment of the interactions of culture and industry in Keith Negus's cultural-studies approach to the rap music industry; and Georgina Born's anthropological study of different types of reflexivity in the BBC. But all these studies, in different ways, argued that media organisations do not operate as independently from the interests of the wealthy and powerful as media workers often claim.

A picture emerges of concentrations of power, reflecting more general concentrations of power in society, but nevertheless limited by a number of factors. Questions of power were explored further in Chapter 3. Here, Jason Toynbee showed how audience market research is seen by some political economists as a means of exerting power over audiences, rather than as a benign way of responding more readily to their audience needs (which is how the media industries prefer to see it). Some political economists, though, stress the changeability of audiences, and the difficulty for media organisations of tracking changes in audience tastes and habits. This emphasis on uncertainty was considerably extended in Ien Ang's Foucauldian approach, which focused on the difficulty of pinning down audiences. Here, by contrast with the political economy approach, attention is drawn to the dispersal rather than the concentration of power.

Gillian Ursell's account in Chapter 4 contrasted a Marxian approach (this time, labour process theory), which has a very strong view of the negative operation of power by businesses (this time with regard to the exploitation of media workers), with a more benign market liberal view, and with a Foucauldian view. This last approach takes a different critical perspective, here bringing in the complicating effects of subjectivity, referring to the way in which power operates *through* subjects, rather than being imposed upon them from above.

In these studies of media production, then, power is understood only in some ways and at some times, as *imposable* on media audiences. The chapters emphasise that power is a set of processes that needs to be looked at from a number of angles in order to understand its complexity. Because power is so complex, some would prefer that we abandon talk of it altogether; however, a great deal of research, including much of that reported in this volume, suggests that when it comes to media production this would be a mistake. For media production is a site where crucial decisions are made regarding social meaning.

Knowledge, values and beliefs

How can we understand the relationships between media producers, on the one hand, and knowledge, values and beliefs on the other? Knowledge, values and beliefs were important to Downey's examination in Chapter 1 of whether ownership, market size and internationalisation matter in the media. For what lies beneath anxieties about these factors is concern about the potential influence being exerted over people's knowledge, values and beliefs. For example, one reason to be worried by the domination by Western countries of global media markets (dubbed 'cultural imperialism' by some) is that this may involve the displacement of non-Western values and beliefs. But Downey showed how critics respond that Western values and beliefs are more varied and pluralistic than the cultural imperialism model suggests.

Chapter 2's focus on the relationship between production organisations and texts makes questions of knowledge, values and beliefs more central still. For example, we saw how the reporting of crime, with its potential to command huge influence over understandings of social punishment, and our knowledge about safety, might be affected both by news values at work among journalists, and by sources with ties to interested groups, such as the police. Media production can, then, be viewed as a site in which values and beliefs are continually in conflict over, for example: how to promote and market which records (in Negus's study of rap); or over whether the emphasis in the BBC should be on 'serving the public' or on financial efficiency (in Born's ethnographic analysis).

Questions of method raise issues concerning knowledge of social processes. Methods were to the fore in Chapter 2, as we surveyed a variety of ways in which research into media organisations has been conducted. Chapter 3 looked at how the media industries themselves research their audiences, and here questions of knowledge were critical. Toynbee showed that claiming knowledge of the audience is a crucial element of the media industries. That gaining such knowledge is a very tricky business therefore has important implications for these industries, and for certain political economy critiques of them. For if such knowledge is provisional and highly dependent upon context, the media industries might be less about 'giving people what they want' than media industry advocates claim; and they might be less monolithically powerful than some critics – including some who take the political economy approach – believe. If this is the case, however, we should certainly not conclude that market research is unimportant; for Toynbee's argument is that market research is an important tool with which media businesses can exercise power over creative workers.

Chapter 4 surveyed a variety of perspectives on media work, and the more sociological approaches (those that study media workers as professionals, and those that look at identity and discourse in relation to media workers) laid great emphasis upon the values associated with work in this sector. For example, for Burns, in his study of the BBC, the very notion of professionalism was 'a moral order', a way of claiming autonomy through the assertion of superior values. Burns, like other sociologists, was keen to show how such values are carefully constructed, with particular interests in mind. Meanwhile, the Foucauldian approach outlined by Ursell shows how certain values associated with the media themselves (as key markers of identity) help to encourage many young people to seek access to the media, ensuring a reservoir of spare labour for this difficult-to-enter business.

As a whole, the chapters show that a reciprocal process is at work between the knowledge, values and beliefs of the social world, on the one hand, and the media, on the other. But different perspectives take different views on this (as with power) – with market liberals taking a more benign view of the way in which markets can produce a diversity of such knowledges, values and beliefs, while critical perspectives tend to have a more gloomy view of media institutions as transmitters of such knowledge, values and beliefs from the more powerful to the less powerful.

Change and continuity

How are change and continuity intertwined in media production? The last century or so has seen a massive growth of media production organisations. Each of the chapters turns its attention to particular aspects of change. In Chapter 1 Downey focused on claims about important changes and their significance, especially the concentration of markets in the hands of a few very large businesses, and internationalisation. In Chapter 2, a number of the studies analysed had important things to say about organisational change: for example, Negus wrote of the way in which black music divisions were opened and closed by corporate parent companies, while Born discussed the effects of the introduction of certain audit procedures in the BBC of the 1990s. Related changes were discussed in Chapter 4, though from very different perspectives: Ursell contrasted the managerialist perspective, which looks for new forms of flexibility from workers in the interests of greater efficiency, productivity and profit, with labour process theory, which interprets such changes as further exploitation. Ursell suggests that the case for labour process analysis is backed up by increasing levels of casualisation among media workers. But she also has criticisms to make of labour process theory: in particular, she says, to interpret such changes as deskilling might not be accurate. Toynbee, meanwhile, in Chapter 3, examined the introduction of new audience research practices in recent decades, as the media industries constantly attempt to 'capture' the audience.

However, while the fast-moving world of the media industries may sometimes appear to be constantly in flux, threads of evidence of important continuities run throughout the chapters. Certain dynamics of the media industries seem to be at play over a long historical span, in particular the uncertainty surrounding what audiences will want and the high levels of risk associated with production (see Chapters 1 and 3). And underlying all this is, of course, the drive to make profit that is characteristic of most businesses, as Ursell emphasised. However, uncertainty and risk do not mean that the corporations which dominate media production are weak compared with producers (and here we return to the theme of power again). Indeed, these dynamics help to favour large corporations in general, and to increase their market share. Over the last few decades the names of the companies dominating the media landscape have changed, reflecting the competitiveness of the media business; even Murdoch's and Berlusconi's companies will one day lose their formidable clout. But while *individual* media businesses may rise and fall, large media corporations have *collectively* increased their power in the realm of media production over the last few decades, including in the vitally important area of media policy.

All of which raises the important question of how to interpret such tangled dynamics of change and continuity, and indeed of power, knowledge, values and beliefs. The main aim of this volume has been to clarify positions that might be taken towards media production. A number of different approaches have been compared and contrasted. The market liberal and social market perspectives tend to dominate governmental thinking. The political economy and Foucauldian positions might be widely held by academic media researchers and activists, but are rarely translated into policy action. But if these political economy and Foucauldian critiques of media production have any validity, and if the media are as important to contemporary life as many analysts claim that they are, then efforts to bring such criticisms into public debates need to be redoubled.

Acknowledgements

Grateful acknowledgement is made to the following sources for permission to reproduce material within this book.

Chapter 1

Figures

Figure 1.1: Copyright © L Cironneau/Associated Press; Figure 1.2: The Road to Serfdom in Cartoon, Originally published in Look magazine, reproduced from a booklet published by General Motors, Detroit in the 'Thought Starter' series (no 118); Figure 1.3: Copyright © Partito Marxista-Leninista Italiano.

Readings

Reading 1.1: Extract from COMMUNICATIONS by Raymond Williams published by Chatto & Windus. Used by permission of The Random House Group Limited; Reading 1.2: from MASS COMMUNICATION AND AMERICAN EMPIRE, 2nd EDITION by HERBERT SCHILLER. Copyright © 1992 by Westview Press, A Member of the Perseus Books Group. Reprinted by permission of Westview press, a member of Perseus Books, L.L.C.

Chapter 2

Figures

Figure 2.1: Copyright © Urlich Baumgarten/Vario Press, Camera Press London; Figure 2.2: Copyright © News International Syndication. Reproduced by permission of News International Syndication Ltd; Figure 2.4: Copyright © MK News; Figure 2.5: Courtesy of the International Gramsci Society; Figure 2.6: Copyright © Mirrorpix; Figure 2.7: Copyright © Mirrorpix; Figure 2.8: Copyright © Remy De La Mauviniere/AP Photo; Figure 2.9: Copyright © BBC.

Readings

Reading 2.3: Negus, K. (1998) Cultural production and the corporation: musical genres and the strategic management of creativity in the US recording industry, Media, Culture & Society, Vol. 20. Reproduced by permission of Sage Publications, Thousand Oaks, London and New Delhi, Copyright © Sage Publications 1998; Reading 2.4: Born, G. (2002) Reflexivity and ambivalence: Culture, Creativity and Government in the BBC, Cultural Values, Vol.6, Nos 1 & 2, Taylor & Francis.

Chapter 3

Figures

Figure 3.1: Hulton Archive/Getty Images; Figure 3.2: Copyright © Getty Images; Figure 3.3: Image courtesy of The Advertising Archives; Figure 3.4: Copyright © Punchstock; Figure 3.5: Copyright © Barrie Wentzell.

Readings

Reading 3.1: from Audience Economics: Media Institutions and the Audience Market Place by Philip M Napoli © 2003 Columbia University Press. Reprinted with the permission of the publisher; Reading 3.2: Dependency Road: Communications, Capitalism, Consciousness, and Canada, Dallas Smythe. Copyright © 1981 by Ablex. Reproduced with permission of Greenwood Publishing Group, Inc., Westport, CT.; Reading 3.4: Ang, I. (1991) Desperately Seeking the Audience, Routledge; Tables 3.1 and 3.2: Copyright © Yahoo! Inc. All Rights reserved.

Chapter 4

Figures

Figure 4.1: Copyright © Warner Bros/Ronald Grant Archive; Figure 4.3: Copyright © BBC; Figure 4.4: Copyright © VT Freeze Frame.

Readings

Reading 4.1: Barnatt, C. and Starkey, K. (1994) The emergence of flexible networks in the UK television industry, British Journal of Management, Vol.5. Blackwell Publishing Ltd; Reading 4.2: Thom, C. (2002) Spoon-fed and overspun, UK Press Gazette, 5 July 2002. Copyright © Cleland Thom. Cleland Thom is director of CTJTS Ltd, one of the UK's largest journalism training organisations.

Cover

Getty Images.

Every effort has been made to contact copyright holders. If any have been inadvertently overlooked the publishers will be pleased to make the necessary arrangements at the first opportunity.

Index